LINC[OLNSHIRE]
VIL[L]AINS

ROGUES, RASCALS AND REPROBATES

LINCOLNSHIRE VILLAINS

ROGUES, RASCALS AND REPROBATES

DOUGLAS WYNN

The History Press

First published 2012

The History Press
The Mill, Brimscombe Port
Stroud, Gloucestershire, GL5 2QG
www.thehistorypress.co.uk

© Douglas Wynn, 2012

The right of Douglas Wynn to be identified as the Author
of this work has been asserted in accordance with the
Copyrights, Designs and Patents Act 1988.

British Library Cataloguing in Publication Data.
A catalogue record for this book is available from the British Library.

ISBN 978 0 7524 6611 8

Typesetting and origination by The History Press
Printed and bound by TJ International Ld, Padstow, Cornwall

Contents

Acknowledgements

As ever I am indebted to a great number of people in the writing of this book and if I have forgotten to mention anyone who has given comments or helpful advice then please accept my apologies.

I am very much obliged to staff at various libraries I have visited, in particular those at Louth, Boston, Grimsby and Lincoln, who have been particularly helpful. I should also like to thank Richard D'Arcy for his continued help with the loan of books, pictures and the immense amount of help with research he has given me. My grateful thanks also go to David Robinson for help with the research and for his useful advice. Also to D.C. Thomson & Co. Ltd, for permission to use a photograph from the *Weekly News*. I am also pleased to thank Norman Cawkwell for allowing me to use pictures from his collection. I should also like to thank Jennifer Briancourt of The History Press for her assistance in the production of this book.

And last but by no means least I should like to thank my dear wife, Rosemary, for all the help and encouragement she has given me, without which this book would never have been completed.

Introduction

Although Lincolnshire is a rural county it has its share of cities and towns, and also its share of villains. Villainy occurs just as often in quiet country villages as it does in towns, and if you've ever visited a remote country store you will know that you have to count your change, just as you would in a big city supermarket.

Any survey of villains needs some sort of classification or it's liable to get very confusing. Is someone who holds vehicles up at gunpoint on the highway a highwayman or a highway robber? Should he appear in the chapter on Highwaymen or that on Robbers? This is not too difficult. I've placed a man who rides a horse and shouts 'Stand and deliver!' as he points his pistol as a highwayman. All the others, sometimes called footpads, I've put in Chapter One, 'Robbery'. But how would you classify John George Haigh, one of the most prolific and fiendish English murderers of the twentieth century? Without his skills as a conman and expertise as a forger he could not have done the things he did. And what about Robert Augustus Delaney? He conned a wealthy widow into marriage, spent her entire fortune and then decamped with her niece, but later became an infamous cat burglar. Or how about the man who made off with a Grimsby trawler and sailed it halfway round the world, until he ran out of fuel and food. Was he a pirate or a robber? Smugglers are comparatively easy to classify, though in bygone times practically everybody was at it and few people were actually caught.

Sadly, we just have to accept that for many villains, 'turning a fast buck', as the saying goes, is the main aim in life. For some, how they come by it is not so important; whether by beating a person over the head to rob them, breaking into a shop, or setting up an elaborate con – whichever is easiest at the time is the deciding factor. I hope this selection of criminal tales will entertain, inform and, possibly, terrify you.

As with all my stories I've tried to stick to the facts, but occasionally I've brought conversations which almost certainly took place at the time up to date. And in some cases I have altered names to avoid distressing those caught up in crimes through no fault of their own.

A Note on Money

Before decimalization, the smallest value coin was the farthing. Four farthings made one penny. There was also a coin for two farthings – a halfpenny; a coin for three pennies and one for six pennies. An old coin was the groat, which went out of circulation in the seventeenth century. It was worth four pennies (or pence). Twelve pennies made one shilling and two shillings made a florin. There was also a coin for half a crown, which was two shillings and six pence, and a crown, which was five shillings. There were twenty shillings in one pound or one sovereign. A guinea was one pound and one shilling. The coin was not used after 1813, but the term remained in use for many years afterwards. It is very difficult to know what an amount of money in bygone times would be worth today, but an idea can be obtained from the website www.eh.net.

Douglas Wynn, 2012

Chapter One

Robbery

The 1856 Rural Police Act compelled local authorities to set up police forces. Before this, policing was on a do-it-yourself basis. If someone assaulted or stole from you it was up to you to go out and find the person who did it. If you were lucky, you might call on the assistance of the local constable. His was a part-time job. He was appointed for a year and, since he wasn't paid, the job was not too popular. He had to see to drunks and vagrants and, if there was a local lock-up, imprison them until he could take them before the local magistrates. If the constable was busy and couldn't help, you had to go to the local Justice of the Peace yourself. If he issued an arrest warrant and the miscreant was caught, you would have to appear with your thief, together with witnesses, and the thief would duly appear with his witnesses. The magistrate would then adjudicate. If the matter was trivial he might decide himself. If not, for example if it was a case of theft, he would refer the matter to a higher court, where several magistrates would sit together, often with a jury. This was the Quarter Sessions, held four times a year. To wait for the next one, the accused would have to find two respectable friends to vouch for him and give sureties of £20 each. It was called being bound over. If the case was more serious, or it was feared the accused might abscond, he would be incarcerated in the local House of Correction.

Assize Court in Lincoln Castle.

At the Quarter Sessions it might be decided not to prosecute or the verdict might go against the accused. If the accused was convicted he could be fined, receive a prison sentence or be flogged, sometimes the last two together. Flogging could be done in the House of Correction, or the culprit would be tied to a horse and cart, stripped to the waist and receive between twenty and twenty-five strokes whilst being dragged through the town. For more serious offences, the accused would be referred to the assizes in Lincoln, which were held twice a year, in Lent (March) and Midsummer (July).

The death penalty could only be imposed by a judge sitting at the assize court. By 1819, hanging was the sentence for 222 offences. Apart from murder, manslaughter, rape, sedition (speaking against the king) and homosexual offences, there were bizarre ones as well. Damaging Westminster Bridge was one, impersonating a Chelsea Pensioner was another, as well as being seen with a sooty face if you were not a 'real' sweep. You could also be hanged for any theft exceeding one shilling (5p in today's money). This was called grand larceny. It had a serious affect on the conduct of prosecutions and juries at Quarter Sessions.

A prison hulk.

Most of them tried to keep the value of the articles stolen at under one shilling. However, receiving the death sentence did not always mean that you would be hanged. Many death sentences were commuted to transportation for life.

Rebecca Bolton (sometimes spelt Boulton) was the wife of Thomas Bolton of Thimbleby. She was in the service of John Grant, who was a grazier at Withcall, near Louth. In May 1784, she left the household early one morning, before anyone was up, taking with her a cotton gown, an apron and a silk hand-kerchief, all of which belonged to the Grant family. When Rebecca did not return, John Grant went to Louth to lodge a complaint with the Justice of the Peace, Bentley Bennett. The magistrate took down particulars and issued a warrant for her arrest. The local constable was informed and he hired a pony with which to go and look for her. Rebecca was eventu-ally tracked down in Keddington and brought back to Louth, where she made a full confession to the magistrate and also said that she had stolen some articles from the other servants. She was charged with petty larceny and sent for trial at the assizes, where she was convicted. Since she had already been

The village of Thimbleby.

The village of Withcall.

before the magistrates in February for stealing some articles of clothing at Stickney, it's possible that she received a heavier sentence than she otherwise would have. At all events, she was sentenced to be transported for seven years.

Prisoners sentenced to be transported were often sent from the gaol at Lincoln to one of the hulks moored in the Thames Estuary or Portsmouth Harbour to wait for a ship to take them to the colonies. Rebecca, however, spent three years in gaol at Lincoln, during which time she gave birth to a baby daughter. She then left England on the *Prince of Wales*, which sailed on 13 May 1787, for New South Wales. It was the first consignment of prisoners to Australia, after the loss of the American colonies, when that source of transportation of prisoners dried up. Eleven ships made the journey in convoy, including six transports carrying 600 convicts each. The voyage took nearly nine months and conditions on the convict ships were appalling. Four convicts, all wearing legs irons, had to share a space

The village of Keddington.

of 6ft (1.8m) by 7ft (2.1m). It was impossible to stand upright and conditions below decks – especially in the heat of the tropics – must have been insupportable. A quarter of the convicts died before they reached their destination, which was near the town of Sydney. Rebecca survived the journey, but died within three months of landing in Australia, her daughter dying soon after.

A Quartet Hanged at Lincoln, 1784

James Raynor and his wife Easter kept a boarding house at Saxilby, about six miles north-west of Lincoln. On Saturday, 13 September 1783, thirty-five-year-old Thomas Wood, who originally came from Yorkshire, and some friends booked in for one night's stay. During the night Mrs Raynor was woken by the sound of a window being broken and a shadowy figure standing by the bed. She screamed, but the man grabbed her and threatened to cut her throat if she didn't keep quiet. The sounds had also woken her husband, James, who sat up in bed, but the man, whom he now recognised as Wood, waved a knife at them and again warned them to keep quiet. They could now hear the sounds of other people moving about in the house.

The pair lay terrified in their bed all night, not daring to move, but in the morning they got up to find that Wood and his friends had gone. Also missing was a silver tankard, a silver pint mug, £15 in cash and some other items. James Raynor went to the local Justice of the Peace and a warrant was issued for the arrest of the men. Thomas Wood was subsequently arrested in Nottingham and brought back to Lincoln. The other men were never found, nor were any of the stolen items. In fact, the only evidence against Wood at his trial at the Lent Assizes on 9 March 1784 was the evidence of Raynor, who said he recognised him. Wood was nevertheless found guilty of grand larceny.

Saxilby High Street.

At the same assizes, twenty-six-year-old Richard Downind from Boston, and twenty-two-year-old William Davison from Stickney, were committed for trial on a charge of having stolen three silver tankards, three silver pint pots and one silver half-pint pot, which together were valued at £20. They belonged to William Thacker of Langrick Ferry, near Boston, who had them locked in a cupboard in his cellar. One night the cellar window was broken, the cupboard door forced open and the silver stolen. A week or so later the silver items, now broken into pieces, were offered by two men to a shopkeeper in Boston. He knew about the robbery and asked the men to return the following day, saying he would have a valuer ready to inspect the silver. The unsuspecting robbers did so and on their return the next day were arrested on the spot. Thacker was able to identify his silver by marks on the pieces, and Downind and Davison were committed for trial. Their defence was that they had seen two men burying the silver in a dung heap and had dug it up themselves to sell. The jury did not believe them and they were convicted.

Twenty-five-year-old Richard Bull was a tenant farmer at Frampton, just south of Boston. He was charged with stealing seven sheep from John Taylor of Kirton, the next village to Frampton. They were three male sheep and four female sheep and he unwisely asked a neighbour to look after them for him. John Taylor soon discovered them and was able to identify them by marks he had put in the fleeces. Bull was tried for sheep stealing and subsequently convicted.

Wood, Downind, Davison and Bull were brought into court on 10 March to be sentenced, and all four received the death penalty. It was thought that because Downind, Davison and Bull had all attempted to escape from the castle prison six weeks before that the judge, Baron Eyre, wanted to make an example of them. James Wood was probably sentenced to death because his robbery had included violence. At about half past ten on the morning of 19 March the four men were taken out of their cells, their leg irons knocked off and their arms tied behind their backs. They were then taken by cart out of

The old square at Kirton.

The Strugglers Inn, just outside the castle walls.

the castle gate to the execution spot – just outside the castle walls, near to where the appropriately named Strugglers Inn public house now stands. The gallows was quite a substantial structure, with a crossbeam which could accommodate four prisoners. The men mounted the steps, nooses were placed around their necks by the two hangmen, and caps were drawn over the faces of each condemned man. Then the steps were pulled away and they were left suspended by the neck until they were dead. This could take up to half an hour and provided a grisly spectacle for the several thousand onlookers.

The two hangmen were actually two convicted horse thieves, Robert Preston and George Green, who had themselves been sentenced to death but reprieved when they agreed to hang the four robbers.

Ructions at the Castle, 1785

The Lent Assizes in Lincoln in 1785 opened on 7 March and, during the course of the trials, twelve death sentences were handed out. Only nine men were actually hanged, the other three were reprieved and transported for life. John Huson was convicted of robbing Thomas Holmes on the highway at Well, near Alford, and stealing a pair of pistols, a pair of boots and 13 shillings (65p) in silver. He was condemned to be hanged. Another street robbery occurred late at night in the area known as the Bail at Lincoln, between The Angel and The White Hart Inn. William Ligburn and George Brown robbed William Cumberland of two guineas in gold and 14 shillings (70p) in silver. Ligburn was condemned to be hanged, but Brown was reprieved. Thomas Rawson was committed on two counts of burglary. He had broken into the house of William Camplin of Bonby, near Brigg, and stole 2½ guineas in gold, some silver, two silver shoe buckles and, three days later, he also burgled the house of John Hunt of Castlethorpe

The village of Well.

and got away with 18½ guineas in gold and a gold ring. He too was given the death penalty.

The others were convicted for beast stealing. William Holdsworth stole a black mare at Partney, and Michael Harrison another black mare, this time at Horncastle. Jonathan Warner stole ten sheep at Pinchbeck and John Wright five ewes at Sibsey. John Palferman was convicted of stealing two heifers at Wildmore Fen, and George Huntingdon managed to steal a milking cow at Skirbeck. All six men were sentenced to death.

A few days after they had been sentenced, seven of the nine convicted men attempted to escape. The attempt appeared to have been well planned, for, at the same time the convicts in the cells attacked the guards, some prisoners who were being held ready for transportation to the hulks also mounted an assault on the chief warder's quarters, which were in the same building. At a prearranged moment, when the turnkey came down to the cells (which were in the cellars of the prison) with two assistants – one with a pitchfork to shake up the straw

The White Hart Inn, Lincoln.

The old barracks in Burton Road, Lincoln.

which the floor was covered with – the seven prisoners threw themselves upon the turnkey and his assistants. They were able to wrest the pitchfork from the grasp of the assistant and use it as a weapon to force the three warders into a corner before tying them up. While this was going on, Michael Harrison, one of the nine convicts condemned to death, managed to scramble up to a higher level and make contact with a debtor convict. He appealed to him to raise the alarm immediately, as the escaping convicts had threatened to kill anyone who stood in their way. The debtor rushed away to raise the alarm, only to find that it had already been done, since the attack on the chief warder's residence had caused the local militia to be called out from their base, which was just up Burton Road.

Two of the escaping convicts fought their way up to the castle yard, but there they were met with the dragoons and rapidly surrendered. They and the rest were placed in double irons and, a few days later, on 18 March 1785, they were taken to the execution site. It seems very unfair that Michael Harrison did not receive a reprieve but joined the others on the gallows.

Horse Stealing, 1789

Mr Stafford was a farmer at Quadring, a village just south of Donnington, which is between Boston and Spalding. He employed a certain John George, whom he found totally unsatisfactory and eventually sacked him. But George was a vindictive man and he was determined to have his revenge. On the night of 31 March he broke into the farmhouse around midnight, when Mr Stafford and his wife were asleep in their beds. When the farmer woke, George savagely attacked him – beating him until he could hardly crawl. Whether this was the main part of his revenge or if he expected to burgle the house as well we do not know, but he only took away a pair of breeches.

To make his escape he also stole one of his former employer's horses and rode out of the county upon it. But whereas a man can hide, it was much more difficult to hide a horse, and when the description of the animal had been circulated it was spotted in Peterborough. A watch was kept on the horse and when George arrived to pick up his steed he was arrested. He was also found to be in possession of Mr Stafford's breeches – they were identified by some papers in the pockets which clearly belonged to the farmer.

John George was taken back to Lincolnshire and came up for trial at the Summer Assizes. The judge pointed out that a lot of the evidence was circumstantial, but nevertheless compelling, and George was convicted of burglary and stealing a horse. He afterwards denied that he had broken into Mr Stafford's house, claiming that he had received the breeches and the horse from someone who had. However, he did acknowledge stealing several horses and, since he was known under aliases, Smith and Flint being among them, it can be assumed that he was an habitual criminal. He went to the gallows on 7 August 1789.

Two Bales of Cloth, 1814

Forty-one-year-old William Ward and thirty-nine-year-old William Bell were general labourers who originally came from Retford. On the night of 12 November 1813, they broke into a draper's shop belonging to D.W. Simpson in the village of Mareham-le-Fen, to the north-east of Coningsby. They stole two bales of cloth valued at £200.

The next day, Mr North, a farmer from the next village, Revesby, discovered that his boat, which he kept at Moorehouses, was missing. He set out to see if he could find it and soon saw it being poled along by two men in a waterway called Newham Drain.

'Hey!' he called. 'That's my boat you've got there.'

'Rubbish!' shouted back one of the men and they continued in the boat, ignoring the farmer. But North kept up with them, walking quickly along the canal bank and continuing to insist that the boat was his, as he could easily recognise it by various markings on the side. When it looked

Mareham-le-Fen village.

as if the farmer was not going to give up, the two men pulled into the bank.

'Well, I will admit that we did find the boat floating free,' said one of the men. 'And we thought that we would take it back to the owner. But we've got rather a lot of parcels and it proved very useful for carting them about. So, if you will tell us where you keep the boat we will return it after we've unloaded the parcels.'

North didn't believe the man, but he thought that he could easily catch up with them again after he had gone to fetch some assistance. So he agreed and went off. But he only went as far as the next farm, a neighbour of his, and the two farmers soon returned, this time with some farmhands and two dogs. They soon caught up with Ward and Bell, for it proved to be them, but when Ward saw the men and the two dogs he pulled out a pistol.

'Keep off. I'll shoot the first man who comes any nearer!' he shouted.

But North bravely came up to the bank. Ward pulled the trigger but the gun misfired and the recoil nearly upset the boat. 'Give it up, Will!' shouted Bell and pulled the boat into the bank. And at that the two men surrendered. When the parcels were opened they were found to contain the missing merchandise.

Ward and Bell went for trial at the assizes on 15 November. They offered the defence that they had been approached by two men in Horncastle to search for a missing boat in the Fens, which contained some goods belonging to them. But the jury didn't believe them and both men were found guilty of burglary and sentenced to death. Bell was later reprieved and sentenced to be transported for life. This was sometimes the case with felons who had not been violent or it could be shown that they had not been carrying arms.

William Ward was executed on 1 April 1814. He was the last person to be executed on the old gallows outside the castle walls. From then on, executions took place either within the

Cobb Hall in Lincoln Castle.

castle walls or on top of Cobb Hall. Ward is said to have been remarkably cool about the whole affair and sucked an orange while waiting to be hanged. The hangman was a convict from Boston, John Blissett, who was waiting to be transported.

A Remarkably Silly Defence, 1815

Thomas Elderkin kept a draper's shop at Pinchbeck. On the night of Friday 14 April he locked up his shop at 9.30 p.m. He went home and returned the following morning to open up again, but this time he had an unpleasant shock. Almost the whole of his stock had disappeared. Someone had broken in and stolen items which were valued at £400. This was a disaster for Elderkin, for it meant that his livelihood had disappeared in one stroke. But he had to do something about it himself, since there was no police force to investigate the robbery for him. He canvassed the neighbours and got a description of two men who had been seen near the shop the previous night, but nobody knew who they were. So Elderkin put up posters in the village and in the nearby town of Spalding, offering a reward for information leading to the arrest of the criminals.

Unfortunately no information was forthcoming. Elderkin was beginning to despair that he would ever find out who robbed his shop. In fact he had to wait for three months before he heard anything useful. Then he had a tip-off. There had been some navvies working nearby. In those days they were called 'bankers' and they were employed mainly to work on the banks of waterways, building canals or widening the existing rivers. A great many of them were from Ireland, but quite a lot had permanent homes in the area. The informant named Thomas Clarke and his friend Henry Coster as likely culprits, and so Elderkin duly collected the local parish constable from Spalding and they went to where Clarke was living at Pode Hole. A search of his house soon turned up many of the stolen items, together with a couple of pistols, shot, saws, drills and pick-locks.

While this was going on, Thomas Clarke, unbeknown to Elderkin and the constable, sent his eleven-year-old son John round to Coster's house at Gosberton to warn him to get rid of anything which might incriminate him. But Coster obviously didn't think that he was in any danger and did nothing about it. He was rather surprised then, when, two days later, Elderkin and the constable turned up at his house. They soon discovered the rest of the stolen goods and Coster, like Clarke, was taken into custody.

Both men appeared at the Summer Assizes in Lincoln that year. Clarke's defence must be one of the silliest on record. He claimed that someone must have put the stolen articles through his back window without him knowing anything about it, because the goods were nothing to do with him. Coster's was not much better. He said that all the items in his house had been paid for, even though Elderkin was able to identify his own property and to repute Coster's suggestion that he had paid for them. The jury took just fifteen minutes to return guilty verdicts and they were both condemned to be hanged.

It soon became obvious to the authorities at the castle where Clarke and Coster were being held that a great many local navvies were coming to see the pair. There were over a thousand men working on the River Witham, within twenty miles of Lincoln, and it was thought that an attempt might be made to rescue the two when they were taken out to be hanged. The execution was due to take place on Friday 28 July, and, on the Wednesday before, two men were seen lying on top of the castle walls, on the south side. They were called upon to surrender and when they refused, were fired upon by the watchmen before making their escape. It was therefore decided to have the execution inside the castle and a temporary gallows was erected just inside the castle gates. The public were still allowed in, but the gallows was surrounded by a ring of soldiers.

The execution went ahead, as planned, at noon. Clarke was sullen, but Coster assured the crowd that he died happy and took off his shoes and threw them into the crowd. The bodies were taken down and handed over to their friends, who took them away for burial, the service being attended by 150 navvies.

Shouts in the Night, 1819

David Plowright kept a lodging house at a rather isolated spot near Spalding. On the night of 24 November 1818, at between one and two o'clock in the morning, he was disturbed by shouting from the street outside and a loud knocking at his door. He opened his bedroom window, which looked out on to the street, and saw below him two young men banging on his front door. When they saw him they shouted, 'We want lodgings for the night!'

'Go away. It's too late,' Plowright shouted back.

But the men refused to leave and continued banging on the front door. Eventually Plowright threw down sixpence (2.5p) and told the men that they could get lodgings in Spalding, just down the road. It wasn't a very clever move as the young men realised the weakness behind the gesture. They demanded more money and continued to pound the front door. By this time Plowright had realised his mistake and was determined to make a stand. He went and got his shotgun, came down the stairs and sat on the bottom step in front of the front door with the gun across his knees.

Young Jemima Peasegood, the maidservant, had also been awakened by the noise and came downstairs to see what the ruckus was all about. Plowright told her and together they sat on the bottom step. By now the noise from outside had increased and it sounded as if someone was taking a hammer to the door panels. Eventually a hole appeared in the door and the barrel of a gun was poked through. Terrified, Plowright told Jemima to give the men what money she could find and he would recompense her later. Then he retreated upstairs, shut and bolted the door at the top of the stairs behind him and went back to bed, shivering with fright.

Meanwhile, Miss Peasegood watched in horror as a hand appeared through the hole in the door and proceeded to unbolt it from the inside. When the door was opened the two young men rushed in. Jemima gave them what money she had – a £1 coin – and asked them to leave. But they only laughed. One of them herded the young girl into the kitchen and proceeded to assault her. Luckily, the other came in and told his friend to stop, as they had come to rob and they should get on with it. The attacker reluctantly agreed and the two then proceeded to ransack the downstairs rooms. Jemima managed to escape out of the back door and hid in the garden until the men had gone. Then she went back into the house and roused Plowright. He came back downstairs, raised the alarm and together they made an assessment of what had been stolen.

The two robbers were soon apprehended. Young Jemima Peasegood had recognised twenty-three-year-old John Louth, and John Parker, aged twenty-one, and a local constable arrested both men at the Cross Keyes public house in Spalding between 11 a.m. and 12 noon that very morning. The constable found a bunch of Plowright's keys on Parker, and when their lodgings were searched, several more items were found, including a silver tea caddy.

Louth and Parker were sent for trial at the Lent Assizes. They offered no defence and were both sentenced to death. However, because Parker had offered no violence and indeed had prevented Louth from assaulting the girl, he was later reprieved.

Robert Delaney, Gentleman Jewel Thief (1891-1948)

The Aswarby S-bend on the A15 between Sleaford and Bourne is a trial for most drivers today, but on a very windy night in October 1927, it was almost a death trap. The wind had blown down a tree, which projected into the road, and a speeding Austin 12 only just missed it, but went out of control and ended up in a ditch on the other side of the road. Two men climbed out, unhurt but very annoyed.

'What the hell do we do now?' complained the younger of the two.

'I don't know!' snapped the other. 'I suppose we'll have to try and find someone to pull us out.'

It was at that moment that another car pulled up beside them, having seen the headlights of the car in the ditch. The older man explained what had happened and the other driver offered to stop off in Sleaford and notify the police.

'Oh, you don't need to bother them,' said the driver of the crashed car hurriedly. 'Just see if you can find a garage open and tell them where we are.'

The other driver nodded and went on his way. But he called at the police station in Sleaford anyway and told them what happened. The local PC at Osbournby, a village only a mile or so south of the Aswarby turn, was notified and he went to the scene of the accident. He was immediately suspicious of the two men. They were rather scruffily dressed to be driving such an expensive car; the younger one had on an old blue suit with a muffler round his neck and the other was similarly attired. PC Allen said he would go and collect a farmer, who would have horses to pull the car out of the ditch. He did so, but he also telephoned Inspector Collison in Sleaford and asked him to attend and see what he thought of the pair.

The Inspector was also suspicious. He asked the older man his name and he replied that it was Mr Collins of Swineshead and his companion was Mr Brown. He said the car was his and he was on his way to Peterborough. But the officer noted that the car was pointing in the wrong direction for Peterborough and he also noted several items on the back seat of the vehicle, a typewriter, a shotgun, and a Boston Hospital collecting box. They eventually got the car out of the ditch and the Inspector asked the two men to come with him to the police station in Sleaford. As they pulled up at a level crossing, the older man pulled out a revolver and attempted to escape, but both he and his companion were eventually overpowered.

They were locked up overnight and eventually came to trial at Derbyshire Assizes on 9 November 1927, charged with breaking into a garage belonging to a Mr Collins of Swineshead and stealing an Austen car valued at £300. They were also accused of breaking into the offices of William Gilding Ltd at Swineshead Fenhouses, a small hamlet a mile or two outside Swineshead, on the same night. Here they stole a safe containing bankers' cheques, National Health Insurance stamps and various other documents, a double-barreled shotgun, a typewriter and the hospital collection box – the whole lot being valued at £6,277 6s. The two men were both convicted; the older man was sentenced to seven years penal servitude and the younger to three years. The older one had, in fact, been released from prison only a fortnight before they embarked on their burglary episode.

His real name was Robert Aloysius Delaney. He was born in Dublin in 1891, but his family, who were quite wealthy, moved to South Africa soon after. In 1915 he joined the army – the South African Heavy Artillery – and was posted to England and stationed near Bexhill-on-Sea, between Hastings and Eastbourne. In the autumn of that year he met Kate Sharpe, who was holidaying in the resort. Delaney, while not tall, was slim, athletic, good looking and had a charming manner, especially with the ladies. He certainly charmed this wealthy widow – she was thirty-six while he was just twenty-four. They were married in December 1915. It seems that Delaney's army career was short-lived as he was posted as a deserter the following month.

Kate Sharpe lived in Woodhall Spa and Delaney joined her there. With his glib promises and his man-of-the-world manner, it was easy for Delaney to get control of his wife's finances. She was the owner of several farms in Lincolnshire and Delaney was able to sell these and, with the cash, he began to live the life of a country gentleman. He took part in many sporting activities and bought a large estate in Swineshead. He and Kate moved into the large house and employed servants, and, for a while, Delaney tried his hand at farming. But he was no businessman and he didn't like hard work either, with the result that most of his business ventures failed. When Kate's first husband died, one of her nieces had come to live with her and she became a companion for Kate. She stayed on when her aunt remarried, looking after the house and the servants. After a time, Delaney began to tire of his wife and turned his attentions to her niece. This culminated in Kate having a nervous breakdown in 1922 and she went away for a period to recuperate. When she returned, she found that Delaney had sold off her estate to pay his debts and run off with her niece, leaving her destitute. She'd never had to work before, but she settled down to work in service and lived in a small cottage in Swineshead. She later moved into a council house in the same village, where she lived until she was ninety-two.

Meanwhile, Delaney and his new 'wife' (he was never divorced from Kate) rented a boarding house in Westcliffe-on-Sea. But Delaney never spent much time there – he often went up to London's West End, where he liked to go to nightclubs and mix with the wealthier clientele. He told Kate's niece these were business trips. As usual he ran out of money, and, not long after, there was a fire at the boarding house. No one was hurt but there was considerable damage. Delaney claimed £2,000 in insurance but received only £400. After this, Kate's niece became fed up with life with Delaney and went home to Swineshead. Delaney tried to get her back; he even travelled to Swineshead to see her, but her family refused him entrance to the house.

Delaney gave up the boarding house and went to live in expensive hotels in London. But his lifestyle required a considerable income, which he did not have. It was around this time that he turned to burglary – becoming a gentleman jewel thief. He mixed with High Society, posing as a Captain Craddock, and took careful note of which jewels titled ladies were wearing. His charming manner often got him invitations to their houses, where he was able to make friends with the servants, particularly the female ones, and learn where their mistresses kept their jewels, as well as the general layout of the house.

Cat burglar Robert Delaney. (Photograph © *Weekly News* D.C. Thomson & Co. Ltd)

Then it was only a question of gaining access to the house. The lower windows would be heavily secured, but the top ones, where the servants' quarters were, would be easier to open. The only problem was that they would be 40 or 50 feet above the ground. Delaney's solution was to climb the drainpipes.

He explained how he did this years later, when he wrote his memoirs for the newspapers, hoping to earn a little money. It must be remembered, however, that Delaney was a first class liar and conman, so his account must be taken with a large amount of salt. He said that when he was at boarding school he would often climb out of his bedroom window at night to visit cinemas and climb back in later, up the drainpipe. When he began his night-time marauding in London he was only in his early thirties and of slim build, so it was not a difficult feat for him to shin up the drainpipe. He also wore evening dress, so if he was stopped by the police they would take him for one of the swells out for an evening's entertainment. The special evening dress shoes he wore were also supple enough for him to get a good leverage on the wall.

His first job was a big house which fronted a mews, where the family kept their cars. He climbed to the top of a wall and, by leaning over, was able to reach a stack pipe. Foot by foot he worked his way up until he was level with one of the top windows, then he swung his leg over to the window ledge. This was the tricky bit. If he slipped he would plunge to certain death on the paving below. But he managed to heave himself onto the ledge. He carried a little gadget – a thin metal object like a putty knife – with which to slide the catch back and open the window. Then he was inside the servants' room. He had planned his entry so that the servants would all be downstairs having their evening meal and he was able to walk out on to the landing without being seen. Then it was downstairs to the lady of the house's room. He already knew where she kept her jewels and when he had pocketed them he calmly walked down the main staircase, opened the front door and sauntered out. He then lit a cigarette in the street outside and hailed a taxi back to his hotel. Back in his hotel room he examined his haul. He had heard of a possible fence and rang up the man, arranged a meeting and unloaded all the jewels for cash. The fence also gave him valuable advice: always work alone, for friends and helpers will give you away.

Delaney made so much money from this first robbery that he was able to take an extensive overseas holiday. But he was soon committing burglary again. He had come to the knowledge of the police, who called him the 'cat burglar' because of his ability to shin up drainpipes and jump from balcony to balcony. He had several successful forays, but he was caught soon after he had burgled Lady Northcote's house in Arlington Street. This time the police discovered his footprint on a high balcony. They found that it corresponded with a special type of dress shoe with very supple soles. They tracked down the shop where these were sold, but the man who had bought them had given a false address. But the police persisted, keeping watch in the bars and clubs in the area, and eventually they got lucky. A man was spotted wearing such shoes. He was followed to a block of flats near Half Moon Street, and, when the police gave the man's description to the lady in charge, she said, 'Why that sounds just like our Captain Craddock.' The flat was searched and a quantity of stolen jewels discovered. Delaney was finally caught, and he went to prison.

He was released early because of good conduct, but decided that London was becoming too hot for him. So he embarked on the disastrous trip to Lincolnshire. He had become friends with an Irishman while in prison in Parkhurst, who was released a few months before Delaney, and together they stole a car in London and drove up to Lincolnshire. They had decided to rob the house where Kate and Delaney had lived in Swineshead, now occupied by a Mr Charles Collins. They left the stolen car at a shed Delaney knew of nearby, walked to the house, broke into the garage and stole the Austen car belonging to Mr Collins. Then they drove it to other premises that Delaney knew of, broke into the offices and stole the safe, which they broke open with a pickaxe. But on their way to Lincoln they had the accident, which resulted in their capture.

Delaney was released on license in 1934 and immediately went back to house-breaking. He was surprised in one house, when he was scooping up the gems, by the butler. Luckily, the man was an old lag and recognised Delaney. He told him to put the jewels back and he would say nothing, so Delaney went away empty-handed. On another job he slipped when the drainpipe became wet through rain and fell, but he managed to catch a window ledge as he dropped and hung on. But he had made a lot of noise and, as he hung in terror, a maid came out of the front door to see what the commotion was. Fortunately for Delaney, she didn't notice him and he was able to slip away.

It was obvious to Delaney he was not as young as he had been and perhaps getting a little old for shinning up drainpipes. So he began to train a sixteen-year-old boy to become a burglar. The boy, who had previously been a milkman, was called Jackie. Delaney took him round to various houses and taught him how to climb up the drainpipes and break in. By this time Delaney had acquired another 'wife'. She called herself Olive Delaney and was some ten years younger than Delaney, and she obviously took some part in his nefarious occupation; when Delaney went to court on 13 November 1934, charged with breaking into a flat at a Kensington Hotel and stealing jewellery worth £1,100, Olive was charged with receiving some of the stolen goods. Although it later transpired that Jackie had climbed up to the fifth-floor flat, Delaney was sent down for nine years.

He spent some of his time in prison on Dartmoor and was eventually released in June 1945. Within a few months of his release he was again before the courts, charged with breaking into a house in Hayward's Heath. Back he went to jail, for four years this time, in Parkhurst. But Delaney was nearing the end of his life. He died in Parkhurst on 13 December 1948, from a heart attack. Apart from for two periods of freedom, since 1927 Delaney had spent the last twenty years in prison.

Chapter Two

Pirates

The picture most of us have today of a pirate is of a fierce-looking man in a cocked hat. He has long hair and sometimes even an eye patch. He wears a short, often brocaded coat with several pistols stuck in his belt, and he waves a wicked-looking cutlass. Sometimes we think of the underlings, the ordinary sea-dog type of pirate, as a man with a cloth over his head, a rough short-sleeved shirt and three quarter length trousers and nothing on his feet. He and his master, the pirate captain, will be concerned with capturing Spanish galleons, pieces of eight, doubloons, buried treasure on tropical islands, and so on.

This sort of picture is largely the result of the romanticization of pirates begun by writers like Byron, with *The Corsair*, and carried on by novelists such as Sir Walter Scott with his novel *The Pirate*, and Robert Louis Stephenson's *Treasure Island*. Then, again in the tradition of children's tales, we have *Peter Pan*. Popular musicals of the Victorian era included *The Pirates of Penzance*, and early films of the last century featured Douglas Fairbanks in *The Black Pirate*, and Errol Flynn in *Captain Blood*.

But even in the seventeenth and eighteenth centuries – sometimes called the Golden Age of Piracy – the reality was very different. Most pirates were exceeding cruel. Any crew

Chests and trunks were brought aboard and ransacked.

or passengers on ships boarded by pirates could expect to be killed. If they were lucky they might simply be thrown overboard to drown. If any of them had information that the pirates wanted they would be tortured. Sometimes, even if they hadn't, they could be dropped from the rigging on to the deck or thrashed with a rope's end, or had their ears cut off just for the pirates' sport. Pirates only kept prisoners if they could be ransomed or were needed to help sail the ship.

Pirate Articles

Pirates often had a code of honour and articles were drawn up setting out what they could or could not do. An example is that of an article drawn up by Captain John Phillips and his crew. Phillips was a ship's carpenter from the West Country. He sailed in a vessel bound for Newfoundland, but the ship was attacked by pirates. Phillips joined them. Later, on the night of 29 August 1723, he and some others secretly boarded a ship in Peter Harbour, Newfoundland, took over the vessel, and sailed it away. He was elected captain of the pirates, and he and his crew set out the following articles:

1. Every man shall obey a civil command; the captain shall have one full share and a half in all prizes; the master, the carpenter, boatswain and gunner shall have one share and a quarter.
2. If any man shall offer to run away, or keep secret from the company, he shall be maroon'd with one bottle of powder, one bottle of water, one small arm and shot.
3. If any man shall steal anything in the company, or game, to the value of a piece of eight, he shall be maroon'd or shot.
4. If at any time we should meet another marooner, that man that shall sign his articles without consent of the company, shall suffer punishment as the captain and the company shall think fit.
5. That man that shall strike another whilst these articles are in place shall receive Moses' Law [40 stripes lacking one].
6. That man that shall snap his arms or smoak tobacco in the hold, without a cap to his pipe, or carry a candle lighted without a lanthorn, shall suffer the same punishment as in the former article.
7. That man that shall not keep his arms clean, fit for an engagement, or neglect his business, shall be cut off from his share and shall suffer such other punishment as the captain and the company shall think fit.
8. If any man shall lose a joint in time of engagement, he shall have 400 pieces of eight; if a limb, 800.
9. If at any time you meet with a prudent woman, that man that offers to meddle with her, without her consent, shall suffer present death.

It seems that Phillips' crew were quite democratic, since they fell out with him the following year, threw him overboard and elected a new captain.

Some piracy, however, was legalised, or at least the authorities cast a blind eye to it. If a country was at war with another, it would allow its own ships to attack those of the enemy. And if the attacked ship was carrying treasure, or other valuable commodities, then it was quite all right to plunder these. Sir Francis Drake famously boasted to Queen Elizabeth I that he would trim the King of Spain's beard, and many Spanish galleons were looted by British sailors during England's war with Spain.

Queen Elizabeth I.

Much piracy over the years has been legitimised in this way, sometimes called legalised privateering. It is said that one of the Greek kings, Philip of Macedonia, encouraged his merchant seamen to engage in piracy in the Mediterranean and took his share in taxes, thereby enabling him to build up a navy. Many other rulers since have made money out of piracy.

Off the coast of Lincolnshire, English vessels attacked those of France, Spain and Holland, during periods when England was at war with them. Notably, this occurred in what is usually called the Hundred Years War with France (1337-1453). At this time there were no galleons loaded with treasure travelling in the North Sea, but piracy went on all the same. The prey was usually smaller vessels, and the cargoes seized were such prosaic commodities as herrings, eels, wool and wine. The mouth of the Humber was a convenient spot for pirates. Ships waiting for the tide to enter the port of Grimsby or to sail further up the river to Hull could be boarded at night and seized.

The boats usually used for this purpose were called balingers. They were small vessels, usually weighing less than 100 tons. They had no forecastle and carried only one sail, either a square sail or one extended on a sprit from the single mast. They had a shallow draught and the early ones could carry up to thirty oars and around forty men. They were fast and maneuverable and were mainly used in coastal trade or as transports. It was reported that in July 1387, merchants Walter Were of Grimsby and Peter Stellar of Hull 'equipped a ship, a balinger and a barge at their own expense to arm themselves against the king's enemies.' Another reason why the mouth of the Humber was important to pirates was the presence there of a village called Ravenserodd.

Ravenserodd

Ravenserodd is one of the 'lost' villages that dotted the east coast of Yorkshire, Lincolnshire and the Humber estuary. Over twenty of these villages – which were thriving communities in medieval times – have been lost to the sea. After a particularly bad storm, which sometimes washes all the sand off Mablethorpe beach, a road can be made out which runs out to sea and used to connect with these lost villages. It is said the ghostly sound of bells can be heard from the church, which disappeared under the waves.

Ravenserodd was located on the tip of the sand and gravel promontory, which curls round like a finger cutting off part of the Humber mouth. The peninsula is called Spurn and still exists today, although not in the same position as it did in the time of Ravenserodd. It has been known since Roman times, and every 200 years or so it disappears to reform later further in towards the coast. A little further up the promontory was the village of Ravenser, which derived its name from the Norse Ravens beach or sandbank, and was the embarkation point for the defeated Scandinavian army, which succumbed to King Harold in 1066. Later, in 1399, Henry of Bolingbroke landed there before he became King Henry IV. Ravenser preceded Ravenserodd, which formed at the tip of the Spurn peninsular around 1234, and people from Ravenser moved there after a ship was wrecked on the sandy point. The village rapidly grew because it was in the ideal position for a port and people there began trading with passing ships. Soon it was overshadowing Grimsby and Hull in importance. In 1260, it had a mayor and over a hundred houses built upon the sand. In 1295, it sent a representative to Parliament, and in 1299 received a Royal Charter to hold a market there. But it didn't last long. In the early years of the fourteenth century, storms began to erode the sand and gravel and people started to leave. Bodies were washed from graveyards and the land rapidly receded.

King Henry IV. (Courtesy Richard D'Arcy)

But there were some people who clung on to the bitter end and these were the pirates. There was no better place in the Humber estuary for a pirate base, with its easy access to the North Sea and the Humber River. But they had to move fast because, in the winter of 1356/7, Ravenserodd finally disappeared altogether.

Grimsby Pirates

With the loss of Ravenserodd the way was open for pirates from Grimsby to take a larger share of the pickings. During the fourteenth and fifteenth centuries, Grimsby was only a small port, lower in importance to Boston, King's Lynn and Hull, but it was admirably placed at the mouth of the Humber, and even ships which were not coming up the Humber would often seek shelter in the estuary. It was, therefore, easy for the Grimsby pirates to choose a target and if that proved too well armed they hadn't far to flee to safety. Although warships might be armed with cannons, commercial vessels very seldom were, and long-range armament usually consisted of bows and arrows. Grimsby was also small enough for captured cargo to be sold there and not to attract too much publicity.

In fact, Grimsby was also a good place for pirates from outside the town to use. In 1405, a ship sailing from Holland to Scarborough with a cargo of herrings was boarded by pirates from Dover, who took the vessel on to Grimsby, where the herrings and the ship were sold. Some years later another Dutch ship, skippered by a John Beaumont, was captured by a pirate ship, which was owned by William Scott of Winchelsea and a fishmonger from London, and taken to Grimsby, where the goods were sold.

All this did not go down well with King Henry VII, who issued a decree declaring that people should not buy from or sell to Danish pirates, who at that time preyed upon French,

Spanish and Portuguese ships. But homegrown pirates were just as active. In 1432, Roger Graynesby and John Edon, incidentally both ex-mayors of Grimsby, were involved in disputes over vessels captured from the French, and, in 1452, a certain Alan Tomlynson claimed that Nicholas Lourance owed him money as part of a ransom for a French sea captain (in those days the captain of a captured vessel was often ransomed), and that Lourance also owed him money for the board and lodging of the Frenchman for thirty-two weeks!

Nicholas Lourance was a servant of Sir John Neville, who owned a number of ships, many of which were involved in piracy. John Neville, Ist Marques of Montague, was an important leader of the Yorkist forces in the Wars of the Roses and was successful in defeating the Lancastrians in the north of England. He was the son of the Earl of Salisbury and the brother of the Archbishop of York. In reward for his victory over the Lancastrians he was made Earl of Northumberland, but later had to give up his title when the Lancastrians came back into favour. He was a very wealthy man and, like many others, was not above a bit of piracy if it brought in some money. He is known to have had ships at Grimsby between 1448 and 1456 and it has been suggested that many, if not most of them, were engaged in piracy. In 1449, Marcus van Calen and other merchants of Bruges complained that their ships were being pillaged by servants of Sir John Neville.

When war broke out between England and Scotland during the reign of Henry VIII, Scottish ships blockaded ports on the east coast. A certain Thomas Demilton from Grimsby tried to run the blockade but his ship was captured by the Scots and taken to Leith, where he was ransomed. Several other Demiltons lived in Grimsby and some were undoubtedly pirates. One was arrested in Grimsby and his ship found to contain gunpowder, ten cannons, pitch and resin to set fire to ships, three crossbows, eight bows and ten sheaves of arrows.

King Henry VIII.

Normally the king was against piracy (unless the country was at war), and his authority was expressed in the Admiralty, who would be expected to try to curb piracy around the shores of England. The Vice-Admiral of Lincolnshire was the Admiralty's representative and held a court in Lincolnshire. This was often at odds with the mayoral courts of Grimsby, which took a much more lenient attitude towards pirates from the town and also to the landing of pirates' plunder, and its subsequent sale in the town, since this increased the economic health of the town. Several cases are on record where foreign owners of plundered ships, which were sold in Grimsby, appealed to the Vice-Admiral and sometimes even the Privy Council for redress.

The mouth of the Humber could be a very dangerous place. A famous case heard in the Star Chamber court occurred in 1525. A ship called the *Jesus*, from the Baltic port of Dantzig, was carrying corn, flax, over eighty barrels of pitch and fourteen barrels of what was called osmonds, now thought to be another name for a type of iron. Taking shelter in the mouth of the Humber she was boarded by French pirates, who took her to Whitby, where her cargo was sold. One of the buyers of the goods was the Abbot of Whitby, John of Hexham, who sometimes used the name Topcliffe. Other buyers included the Conyers family (a very wealthy local family), and several other Whitby townspeople.

The Hull Connection

In 1549, a Grimsby pirate ship, the *Rose*, teamed up with a pirate ship from Hull, the *Michael*, to attack a ship from Amsterdam. The spoils were taken to Grimsby to be sold, and the owners instructed a Hull solicitor to look after their interests, presumably in an attempt to buy back their own goods. Pirates from Hull and Grimsby often collaborated: although Hull was a much bigger port than Grimsby and there was inevitable competition between the two for trade, it was often advantageous for two or more pirate ships to join together to attack merchant ships.

Sometimes pirates from Hull worked with pirates from further afield. In 1369, the Hull ship *Michael* was working with other pirate ships from Blakeney, Yarmouth, Ipswich and Sandwich to attack French ships off the Isle of Wight. On a Friday night in July, a Breton ship was anchored off a creek in the Isle of Wight when she was approached by a boat rowed over from the Hull ship. The Hull men asked the master, William Grysele, to come aboard and have a drink with them and he did so. But while his back was turned one of the Hull men struck him with an axe. They then threw him overboard, boarded the Breton ship and slaughtered all the crew. They took away everything they could carry.

Piracy was indulged in by some of the wealthiest men in Hull. John Tutbury, who later became mayor, received a licence in 1400 to attack Scottish ships, since they were then the king's enemies, and this was renewed in 1402. He and his ship *Petre*, together with another wealthy man of Hull, William Terry, in his ship *George*, attacked the ship of Martin Garschowe of Lübeck and plundered the cargo, which they took to Grimsby to sell. But some Hull merchants themselves suffered from piracy. In 1434, William Thorne was in his ship *Trinity* and was homeward bound from Lisbon with a cargo of wine and oil when he was attacked by French pirates from St Malo and Mont-sur-Michel. They were 400 strong and they boarded the *Trinity* and killed four of the crew and held ten to ransom for 260 marks (a mark was worth about 164 pence or 13 shillings and 4 pence). The money had to be paid by the following Whitsun or the hostages would be put to death.

As in Grimsby, feudal lords were not above indulging in piracy. Lord Tailboys and Sir John Neville were both suspected of piracy and Sir William Ryder's ship *Giles* captured a Spanish ship in 1458 bound for Hull with a cargo of wine and iron. Sir John Neville also kept a balinger at Hull. In 1464, her crew robbed the *Peel* of York and a Dutch ship, the *Gertrude*, wounding one of the sailors of the Dutch ship. They also cut the ship's cable, leaving her to drift dangerously in the haven. They seemingly thought that this was not enough mischief for one night so they broke into a house in Hull and stole some cloth. They were soon arrested, but the magistrates realised whose servants they were and offered to release them if they promised to keep the peace. But they refused. Sir John was furious when he heard about their arrest and wrote an arrogant letter to the magistrates, saying that he should have been allowed to deal with his own men. Even though he had no jurisdiction in the city, the magistrates sent a conciliatory reply and the men were released. This shows how leniently pirates were treated if they were brought before the magistrates. The fine for piracy at the time was 40 shillings, about the same as levied for the adulteration of flour.

Gradually, the feeling against piracy in the Humber began to change. Many Hull merchants were continually loosing valuable cargoes to pirates and with no permanent English navy, with armed warships to patrol the coast, they decided to do something about it. In August 1577, the magistrates from Hull, with a commission from the Lord High Admiral, bought and prepared two ships – the *White Hind* and the *Salamon* – to operate against pirates. The project had an immediate success. Within a week they had cornered a pirate ship in Ingomels Creek, a common haunt of pirates known as Thieves Creek, near Skegness. The ship was the *Elizabeth*, captained by the notorious pirate Lancelot Greenwell. She had a crew of eighteen and was well armed. The crew were taken to Hull and tried before the magistrates and the Earl of Huntingdon, who came especially to be present at the trial. Three of the crew were acquitted but fifteen were convicted of piracy and hanged together in what has become probably the most gruesome spectacle in Hull's history. In addition, the bodies of six pirates were hung in chains at various places along the Humber riverbank.

Piracy in Modern Times

Piracy continues to this day. The newspapers often contain stories of small boats being attacked by pirates in the Indian Ocean and their crews being held for ransom, and a few years ago the Mediterranean had its share of pirates: tour operators were cancelling sailing holidays off the coast of Corfu because of attacks by heavily armed Albanian pirates. Fortunately, there have not been many recent reports of piracy off the Lincolnshire coast and in the Humber, although an interesting case occurred in 1936, which received worldwide coverage and remained a sensation for many years afterwards.

On the morning of 1 April 1936, the trawler *Girl Pat* slipped her moorings in Grimsby Harbour and set out into the North Sea for a fishing trip, which would have lasted about a fortnight. She was average for fishing trawlers at the time, being about 25 tons and 100ft long. And she was relatively new, having only been in service of the Marstrand Fishing Company of Grimsby for a year. The skipper was George Black Orsborne, usually known as 'Dod' Orsborne. He had been born in 1904 and joined the Navy when he was fourteen, claiming to be seventeen and a half, and just saw the end of the First World War, where he was wounded in the Battle of Zeebrugge. The following year he left the Navy and worked on a farm, but his restless spirit persuaded him back to the sea and he eventually became a deck hand on a trawler, rising to become a skipper. His employers later said of him that he was one of the best fishing skippers they had ever had.

However, when Skipper Orsborne set out for the Dogger Banks in the *Girl Pat* that day in April, fishing was not on his mind. For a start he had stowed away his twin brother, James, on board the ship and James was no seaman, having been a grocer in Grimsby. He had also included a man called Stone as mate, although Stone did not have a mate's certificate. Also aboard were two others, Harris and Stevens, and an engineer called Jefferson, who had been included at the insistence of the employers. In fact, Skipper Orsborne did not go fishing, but steered south. This must have caused some consternation to Jefferson, who expected them to start trawling, but when they put in at Dover the skipper managed to give Jefferson the slip when they landed and when the engineer returned to the ship, he found it had gone.

They next anchored off Jersey and took on supplies, and then set off for the Bay of Biscay and landed at Corcubion, in northern Spain. Here they took on more supplies and also had some much needed repairs done, which they debited to the Marstrand Fishing Company. It must be remembered that the small Grimsby trawler was not intended for long sea voyages and probably suffered damage crossing the Bay of Biscay, notorious for rough seas. In addition, the only charts they had with them were for the North Sea. For the rest of the journey they had to rely on Skipper Orsborne's young son's school atlas.

They left Corcubion on 24 April and continued south. By this time they should have been back in Grimsby, and the owners were concerned about what had happened to their vessel. They got in touch with Lloyds of London and a search was mounted for the missing ship. But the next sighting was some three weeks later, when they were seen at anchor off the Salvage Islands, some 17 miles south of Madeira. The Lloyds agent in Las Palmas was notified and he went to investigate, but though he saw the vessel, they evaded him and slipped off. But their lack of proper charts began to work to their disadvantage. Off the west coast of Africa they were twice stranded on sand bars 45 miles off the shore, and had to resort to getting into the small rowing boat to try and pull the vessel off the shoals. They were also down to four bottles of water, some pancakes and a couple of tins of food. All aboard suffered with the tremendous heat of the tropics, but Stone became quite ill and they decided to put into Dakar, further down the West African coast in Senegal.

They reached Dakar on 26 May. Stone went into hospital there and was subsequently returned to England. Skipper Orsborne realised that a great many people would be looking for them and he decided to disguise the vessel as best he could. When at sea he had the name painted out and a new name substituted, the *Margaret Harold*. But a few days later she was spotted by a French liner further south off the coast of Guinea, still heading south. It is possible that Skipper Orsborne wanted to put in to the Azores to stock up with food, water and fuel, but the limitations of the school atlas showed itself again and many days later a small vessel showing a distress flag was spotted by the *Lorraine Cross* off the coast of French Guiana, on the northern coast of South America. But when the *Lorraine Cross* answered their distress call and asked to see documents, the crew of the small vessel hoisted a sail and sailed off.

But the end was not far away. A few days later they were spotted within the three-mile limit of British Guiana. A police launch approached, but was threatened with sinking if they came any nearer. Eventually the launch chased the trawler out to sea, and after about twelve miles the *Girl Pat* ran out of fuel and surrendered. She and her crew were taken to Georgetown, where Skipper Orsborne and his brother were arrested. By this time they were celebrities. The world's press had been following the adventures of the little craft and Orsborne was offered £5,000 – a huge sum for those days – for his story. He subsequently wrote a book on his exploits.

But he had stolen a vessel and he and his brother were brought back to England and charged at Bow Street. The defence put forward for them was rather unfair. They claimed to have had permission from the owners to take the vessel and subsequently scuttle it as part of an insurance fraud. This preposterous suggestion was taken up by the newspapers and caused the Marstrand Company much distress and annoyance. They subsequently sued the newspapers and won substantial damages. The *Girl Pat* was brought back to England and exhibited in various locations to raise money for charity.

Skipper Osborne was convicted of stealing the trawler but received only eighteen months in prison with hard labour, while his brother James received twelve months. So, was he a pirate, or simply a man with a taste for adventure? Who knows?

Another more modern case was reported in *The Times* in 1966. Early on Saturday, 9 July 1966, a fishing vessel left the docks at Grimsby to sail to the fishing grounds in the North Sea. The vessel was the trawler *Loveden*, owned by E. Bacon and Co., and carried a crew of ten – the skipper, the mate, the chief engineer, an engineer, the cook and five deck hands. During the afternoon it was noticed that the deck hands were drinking both beer and wine. This was a bit surprising, as they were only allowed a measure of beer on the trip and they must have brought the wine on board with them. They continued drinking for most of that warm afternoon and by the end of it many of them were obviously the worse for drink.

At about five o'clock one of the deck hands went to see the skipper, who was in the wireless room, and asked if he would send a message to the man's mother. The skipper said he would and had turned to call up Radio Humberside when the seamen grabbed him from behind. The skipper struggled but was overpowered when the crewmember called for assistance and two more deck hands rushed in. They bound and gagged him and bundled him into his own cabin, where he was laid trussed and bound on his bunk. A message sent to the cook that the skipper wanted to see him brought him up to the bridge, where he too was overpowered and put in the skipper's cabin. But the cook managed to free himself and released the skipper, who crept into the wireless room and sent a SOS message before he was discovered and again tied up. He and the cook had ropes placed round their necks and were carted off to the forward hold, where the fishing nets were stored, and confined there in the darkness for several hours. The mate was similarly captured and he too joined the others in the forward hold.

When the look-out sighted land (the German coast), the 'pirates' lowered a lifeboat and rowed for the shore. They took with them 2,540 cigarettes, forty cigars, 5¾lbs of tobacco, a gross of matches, 192 bottles of beer and five gallons of paraffin.

They also stole a pair of binoculars, an electric drill and an electric torch, various provisions and £10 15s in old money. When they had left the ship, the skipper, the mate and the cook were released by the chief engineer. The five men who had left in the lifeboat were soon picked up by German police and taken before magistrates in Bremerhaven, before being extradited to England.

The five men went on trial at Buckingham Assizes in Aylesbury in October 1966, charged with piracy. One man was acquitted as not having taken part in the assaults and the robberies, but the other four were convicted and given long prison sentences.

Chapter Three

Highwaymen

A cart rumbled slowly along the crowded street. In it sat a manacled man, his legs secured by irons. He was Jack Bird, aged forty-two, a notorious highwayman and, on Wednesday, 12 March 1690, he was on his way to Tyburn to be hanged. The cart was followed on its way by laughing children and the crowds who lined both sides of the narrow thoroughfare cheered and waved their arms, kerchiefs and anything else that came to hand. For this was an occasion and the man who was to be hanged was a celebrity. He had been visited in the condemned cell at Newgate Prison by a succession of fashionable ladies about town, and the buildings which overlooked the scaffold, known as Tyburn Tree, were booked up weeks ahead by those anxious to obtain a good view of the spectacle.

Jack Bird was not one of the best-known highwaymen, but even he was rated a considerable celebrity. Highwaymen were the most celebrated of all thieves, vagabonds and villains. Broadsheets printed at the time of their executions gave the story of their lives, poems were written about them, and songs composed and sung in their honour. The historian Macaulay pronounced: 'the English highwayman holds an aristocratic position in the community of thieves'.

Why did they have this romantic aura that set them apart from the ordinary run of evildoers? Mostly they were just ordinary men – and the occasional woman – who would steal anything they could, given the chance. Stealing from shops and inns, for example, if they stayed there, was quite common among them. And once they were out on the road or the heath they would usually be riding a stolen horse. Were they really the romantic figures portrayed in the ballads, where the masked and mounted figure would hold up a coach by firing in the air, doffing his hat as he invited the ladies and gentlemen passengers to disembark and hand over their valuables? The answer is no. A Scottish highwayman well known for his cruelty once held up a judge on his way to the assizes. Finding the judge's servants reluctant to hand over the cash, he forced two to strip, bound them with rope and threw them into a nearby river to drown. Then he hanged the judge! A certain Captain Evan Evans became so annoyed when he found that the man he robbed had only five pence on him, that he thrashed the man to within an inch of his life. A woman who was held up by the well-known highwayman William Cady quickly swallowed her wedding ring. It availed her little. Cady shot her and cut open her stomach to retrieve the jewel.

So how did such routine cruelty come to be so romanticised? The answer consists of many parts. First the very act of holding up a stagecoach was considered to be an act of bravery, although in many ways it wasn't. Highwaymen rarely worked alone and often had companions to help subdue and terrify passengers. And most of them were armed with pistols, which they were quite willing to use. Any awkwardness on the part of the coach driver or the passengers could be curbed by a shot in the head. And since in the Middle Ages roads between towns and villages were rudimentary if they existed at all, and were lonely and unfrequented, especially at night, holding up a coach was a relatively safe thing to do. Unless accompanied by soldiers, coach passengers and coach drivers were rarely armed. And since it was only the relatively wealthy who could afford stagecoach travel anyway, the passengers could usually be relied on to have plenty of cash or valuables with them.

The poor, therefore, would be very unlikely to meet a highwayman. And a man who only robbed the rich would be likely to have a certain appeal to the less well off. They might regard him in a sympathetic light and, since he lived a dashing devil-may-care sort of life, far removed from most people's humdrum lives, this might have a romantic appeal. Having said that, their lives were relatively short. Usually monetary rewards were offered for information leading to their capture and this meant that in the end someone was liable to shop them and they would end up on the gallows.

★★★

In this chapter I have concentrated on the more well-known highwaymen who rode horses and held up stagecoaches for a living. Highway robbery is a term applied to all kinds of roguery practiced outside in streets and on the open road, and is well illustrated by the following story, which comes from the diary of Abraham de la Pryme (1671-1704), an English writer who was born at Hatfield, near Doncaster.

He relates that he heard the story from a friend who knew a farmer in Wroot, near Epworth in Lincolnshire, called Parrel. This gentleman had a big, strong manservant named John, who was not regarded as being very bright. John came to him one day and complained that his wages were not sufficient for the hard work he did and he was thinking of turning padder (becoming a footpad) on the highway. Mr Parrel tried to persuade him not to do it, saying that it was a harder life than the one he had now. But John would not be deterred and set off to try his luck on the Great North Road, between Newark and Grantham, armed with a stout club. Soon he was overtaken by a smartly dressed man riding a horse. As the man went by, John caught hold of the horse's bridle and shouted, 'Stand and Deliver' as he'd heard other highwaymen do.

But the man laughed and pulled out a pistol and pointed it at John. 'Listen to me young man. I am a highwayman myself and you are either a fool, or you haven't been at this game long.'

John hung his head and admitted that it was his first attempt. The man nodded his head. 'Let me give you some advice. When you want to rob a man, don't take hold of his bridle and tell him to stand and deliver, first of all knock him down off his horse. And if he should say anything, hit him again and tell him to shut up. That way you'll soon have him at your mercy.' The man continued to give advice to the poor simple John as they walked together along the road. Then they came to a part of the road which was extremely muddy and churned up and John said, 'I know this part of the country. There's a much dryer way for you and your horse if you go through this field gate and cut along by the side of the field behind the hedge. Then a bit further along you'll come to a gap in the hedge and you can come through that back on to the road.'

The highwayman thanked John and took his advice. But the hedge was very tall and even on his horse he couldn't see over it. When he reached the gap in the hedge, John was waiting behind it with the club in his hand. When the highwayman came through the gap John swung the club and knocked the man off his horse.

'You rogue!' the man shouted. 'Is this how you repay me for all the good advice I've given you?' But John hit him again and told him to shut up. He then searched the man and took £50 from his pockets. Then, leaving the highwayman in the ditch, he jumped on his horse and rode off quickly. When he reached Mr Parrel's farm, he said, 'Sir. You were right about it being a difficult trade to take up and I shan't do it anymore.

Still I've got £50 and a good horse and since I got them from a highwayman, he's not likely to complain to the authorities that he's been robbed!'

Gamaliel Ratsey, 1605

Gamaliel Ratsey, sometimes known as Gamaliel Hobgoblin, was born in Market Deeping, and was the son of Richard Ratsey, a wealthy merchant in the town. Little is known about his early life, except that it is recorded that he 'took to evil courses as a boy'. He joined the army in 1600 and saw service with Sir Charles Blount in Ireland. He was demobbed in 1603 and returned to England. It was a turbulent time in English history. Elizabeth I had just died and been replaced by James I. There had been a series of bad harvests in the country, and jobs for young men were scarce. Gamaliel was one of many young men who had been trained in the use of arms and seen violence in skirmishes with enemy forces overseas, and, returning to peacetime, found that there was little they could do to earn some money. So, many turned to the trade they knew and became highwaymen.

Ratsey first came to notice when he robbed the landlady of an inn at Spalding of £40. This was very large sum in those days and the authorities were soon after him. He was apprehended and sent to prison to await trial. The penalty for such a crime in those days was death by hanging and he was lucky that his career did not end there; he managed to escape, it is said, wearing nothing but a shirt. He subsequently stole a horse and became a highwayman proper. At first he appeared to have worked on his own in the area he knew best, in southern Lincolnshire, but finding that the pickings were only meager (being only able to hold up single travelers or stagecoaches with few people in them), he began operating in Northamptonshire and joined up with two thieves called Snell and Shorthouse.

Their exploits soon became well known. Ratsey, as the leader, was renowned for his daring and also for his humour. He is said to have held up a Cambridge scholar and, because the man seemed to have little in his purse, demanded that he gave a learned oration. In the same way he once forced an actor to recite a passage from *Hamlet* at the roadside. He also wore a mask of hideous aspect to disguise himself and no doubt to frighten his victims further and reduce the likelihood that they would give him any trouble. This gave him the nickname of Gamaliel Hobgoblin. Stories of his exploits began to appear in verse and in song, and most insisted that he always gave money to the poor. However, Ratsey's career as a highwayman did not last long. His two colleagues were captured before he was and to save their necks turned King's Evidence and betrayed him to the authorities. He was captured, tried at Bedford and hanged there on 26 March 1606.

Gamaliel Ratsey acquired some literary significance when Ben Johnson wrote in *The Alchemist* of a 'face cut worse than Gamaliel Ratsey's'.

Jack Bird, 1690

Jack Bird was born in Stainforth in 1648. His parents must have been fairly wealthy since he was sent to school, which in those days would have cost money. When he left school he was apprenticed to a baker in Godmanchester, near Huntingdon, but he stayed only three years before running away. He came back to Lincolnshire and enlisted in the footguards in Lincoln. He was sent to fight in the Low Countries in an army under the command of the Duke of Monmouth, who was later beheaded for rebellion, and took part in the siege of Maastricht in 1617. Having decided that the life of a soldier for five pence a day was not for him, he deserted and made his way to Amsterdam, but not being able to speak a word of the language put him at a disadvantage. He tried to get a little money by stealing, but foolishly stole a piece of silk from a stall. The stall-holder saw him, gave the alarm and he was pursued and quickly caught. He was taken before a magistrate, convicted of stealing and sentenced to twelve months hard labour in prison.

But Jack Bird was not used to such hard work and, being inherently lazy, he tried to avoid it by pretending to be ill. But his gaolers would have none of it. They had a way of dealing with prisoners who were reluctant to work. He was placed in a large empty water cistern and chained to the floor by one foot. Then various cocks were opened to allow water to pour into the vessel. He was given a pump by which he could remove the water, but he had to pump hard to prevent the water coming up, covering his head and drowning him. He was forced to keep this up for an hour, after which he was taken out of the cistern. It was a lesson which Bird learned quickly and he gave no further trouble, completing his sentence without more ado. Then he was deported back to England.

But the lure of easy riches and the adventure of the open road soon tempted him into becoming a highwayman. He collected some pistols and a sword, stole a horse and began his operations on the road between Chatham and Gravesend. He soon spotted a man coming along the road on a horse. The man appeared to be holding the reins awkwardly, but Bird had no compunction and drew his pistol, leveled it and gave the time-honoured salutation. The man pulled up obediently and explained to Jack that he had no hands. In fact, he was a Mr Joseph Pinnis, a riverboat pilot who specialised in piloting ships up the Thames to London. He had previously been a sailor and had lost both hands in an explosion during a naval battle. He had also just come from the docks, having been paid £10 for piloting a Dutch vessel up the river, and thus was a good catch. Mr Pinnis explained all this to Jack Bird and said that since he had no hands, Jack would have to search him for his money.

Jack pulled up close and leaned across to go through the pilot's pockets. But as he did so the man grasped him firmly round the neck with his stumps and pulled him off his horse. Then, jumping off his own horse, he hurled Jack to the ground and fell on top of him. He was a heavy man and he completely overwhelmed the highwayman, who struggled fiercely underneath him. But he couldn't shift the pilot, who was able to rake him with his spurs. They rolled about on the ground until other travelers arrived and helped to secure Jack.

He was committed to Maidstone Prison and remained there until the next assizes. At his trial, he pleaded that it was his first offence and gave his war service in mitigation. But it didn't help that he had been posted as a deserter. However, Jack was luckily in that he was spared the scaffold and sentenced to a long period of imprisonment. When he was released he tried going straight, but found that people would not employ him when they found out he had been in prison, and the menial jobs he did get were not enough to furnish him in the style he wished to live, so it was back to the highway again. Most of his operations seemed to be around London and, soon after he had started again, he met a Welsh drover just north of Acton, which in those days was a village just outside London. The man was on foot while Jack was mounted, but he swung his horse round and pointed his pistol at the man, delivering the usual challenge. But the Welshman, showing remarkable courage, stepped up to Jack's horse and seized the highwayman by the leg, pulling him to the ground. Then he began to belabour him with a short staff he carried. Jack tried to roll out of the way and eventually managed to run round the other side of his horse, followed by the persistent drover. Jack began to think that the situation was reminiscent of the encounter he had with the river pilot all those years before. But prison had hardened him and he now had much less of a conscience. When he could get free of the Welshman's blows, he drew one of the pistols he carried in his belt and shot the man through the body. The man slumped to the ground. Jack quickly searched his victim but discovered only eighteen pence. He then got on his horse and rode off, leaving the man to die by the side of the road.

After this he had more success in his robbery and soon had a reputation around the capital city as a brave but ruthless highwayman. Tales began to be told about him, the most famous one concerning his meeting with an Earl. This titled gentleman was riding in a coach on the Great North Road, just outside London. Jack rode up and, brandishing a pair of pistols, shouted his usual command. The coach drew to a halt and the passengers dismounted at Jack's command. It turned out that the noble lord had his chaplain with him, as well as the coachman and one footman. But Jack was not deterred by the numbers. Now he was quite prepared to shoot anybody who came near him and he raised his guns menacingly. But the lord stepped forward, holding up his hands in a placating way. He was well known for his unconventional behaviour and had often been called 'mad'.

'You certainly have the drop on us and can take all our money. But are you man enough to fight for it?'

'Don't talk such nonsense!' shouted Jack and he pointed the pistols at the Earl.

'Don't get yourself all het-up, friend. I mean no harm. But without your pistols I wonder if you would stand up to me, man to man.'

Jack laughed. 'Me, put my pistols down and all your servants rush on me and beat me to a pulp? I don't think so.'

'No. No. I give you my word as a gentleman. They will all stay out of it. It will be just you and me.' And he turned to his astonished servants standing in a group behind him and told them not to interfere. Then he took off his coat and rolled up his sleeves. 'There you are then. I will box you fairly for all the money I have. If you beat me you take it. If I beat you, you ride off with nothing. Is that fair?'

Jack cautiously slid down off his horse and, keeping an eye on the lord and his servants, holstered his pistols and took off his own coat. As he did so, the chaplain stepped forward and kneeled at his lord's feet. 'Please, your lordship. Do not fight this man on the public highway. Do not demean yourself. Let me fight him instead.'

The Earl looked round at Jack. 'It is up to the gentleman with the guns.'

Jack shrugged his shoulders. 'I don't mind who it is. So long as it's only one at a time.'

And so it was agreed. The chaplain took of his coat and squared up to Jack. But in a few minutes it was obvious that he was no match for the younger highwayman. Jack beat him serverely until the cleric sank to the ground, crying that he could fight no more. The highwayman stood aside getting his breath back, but keeping a wary eye on the rest. Eventually he said, 'Right, now if your lordship will step up I will take you on too.'

But the Earl shook his head, 'Oh no, my man. You've beaten him fair and square and you would certainly beat me as well. Take your money and go.'

Jack Bird did not visit Lincolnshire much. He lived mostly in London, for it was there the opportunities for a highwayman were much greater. The roads leading to and on the outskirts of the capital city were ideal places to ambush travelers who would be likely to be carrying cash or jewellery. And the hovels and slums of the city were ideal places to hide out from whatever policing there was. So it comes as no surprise to learn that the rogue got married in London. His bride was a servant girl to a dyer who lived and worked near the Exeter Exchange in the Strand. But because Jack's occupation led him to have a great deal of money at times and little money at others, he would on occasion spend a great deal of time in pubs and alehouses and consort with prostitutes and ladies of easy virtue.

One particular night in 1690, he was with a woman in the Strand. Seeing another man reeling about and guessing that he was drunk, Bird seized the opportunity of getting a few easy guineas. He attacked the man, but his victim was not so far gone as all that. He began shouting that he was being murdered. This attracted a crowd and though Jack managed to slip away with his loot, his lady friend did not. She was captured, handed over to the watch and finished up in Newgate. Even being associated with robbery of this kind was a hanging offence and Jack went to see the prosecutor to enquire if a few pounds placed in the right hands might alleviate the offence. But unfortunately for him he was recognised and clapped in irons. At the trial he took all the blame, claiming that the woman was an innocent bystander. He was convicted and sentenced to death, being hanged on 12 March 1690 at Tyburn. Afterwards, his body was taken to Surgeons Hall, o be dissected for the benefit of medical students, which was the usual practice with felons.

Tim Buckley, 1701

Tim Buckley is the first Lincolnshire villain this author has come across to be 'burned in the hand'. Branding was very common and continued until the early nineteenth century. If the convicted felon was ordered to be branded by the judge, then the sentence was usually carried out by the local hangman. A couple of iron grips set into the wall of the dock held the left hand in place and a hot iron with the letters V for vagabond, M for malefactor etc. was pressed into the flesh at the base of the thumb. In severe cases branding could be done on the cheeks of the face.

Tim Buckley is generally considered to be one of the worst of career criminals, with few redeeming features. He was born in Stamford in 1672, and later apprenticed to a shoemaker.

He managed to stick at this for three years before running away from his master and making his way to London. There he joined a group of tearaways and layabouts who made a living thieving from almost everybody, including shopkeepers and householders. They even attacked people they found wandering the streets at night. As is usual with criminals of this type, they were either destitute or flush with money, and when they had plenty they spent most of it in a convenient alehouse. At one of these, a favourite with Tim Buckley, he asked the proprietor for a loan of 10 shillings. The man sensibly refused him. But Buckley had a fierce temper and a vindictive streak. Waiting until the middle of the night, Tim and some of his cronies broke into the house and, surprising the innkeeper, his wife and the maidservant in their beds, tied them up and ransacked the house. They got away with the proprietor's life savings – some £40 – as well as three silver tankards, a silver watch and eight gold rings. Soon after, Buckley attacked a man at night near Hyde Park Corner. The victim was quite a well-known character, having literary pretensions, but that didn't prevent Tim robbing him of six guineas and a gold watch.

All this couldn't go on indefinitely and a local constable became suspicious of Buckley and his companions. Local constables were not full-time policemen; they usually served only for a year and the job was unpaid. It was not a popular occupation but public-spirited local businessmen were often persuaded to serve. This particular constable was a baker in the parish of St Giles-in-the-Fields, and he singled out Tim and threatened to pursue him and seriously curtail his activities. But Tim made a bargain with him. If the constable would leave him alone he would join the army. This he did and soon found himself serving with the colours in Flanders. But life in the muddy fields of the Low Countries did not suit Buckley at all – he quickly deserted and made his way back to England.

Sometime later he chanced to meet the constable's wife near Hampstead Heath. She was alone and Tim, making sure there was nobody else around, jumped upon her and dragged her off her horse. Though she screamed he dragged her into some bushes and forced her to the ground. Then, taking out his pistol he pointed it at her and said that he would as soon kill her as not. Taking advantage of the terrified woman he raped her and, to add insult to injury, stole her money, some 11 shillings, and a couple of gold rings, and told her to go back to her husband and tell him who had attacked her.

After this, Tim Buckley decided to make himself scarce in the London area and took himself off to Buckinghamshire. There he managed to steal a horse and became a fully-fledged highwayman. He seems to have operated to the north of London, for there were many reports of his assaults in this area. Among the most notable of these was his ambushing of a certain pawnbroker who had lived in the Drury Lane area, quite close to where Buckley had lived. Tim had a grudge against the man, blaming him for selling on articles Buckley had pawned with him, thus not allowing him to redeem them. With a pistol pointed at him and seeing the angry eyes behind it the poor man gave up without a struggle and parted with 28 guineas, a gold watch, a silver tobacco box and several gold rings.

Another encounter with a man to whom Buckley owed vengeance came in the same area. This time the man was a stock-jobber – these were people who gambled in Exchange Alley; in what is now known as the City of London. The term apparently applies to dishonest practices, but this particular stock-jobber seems to have been a very wealthy man. He had also been in contact with Buckley before, having been responsible for him being convicted of a felony, which resulted in Buckley being branded on the hand. Buckley, therefore, owed him considerable animosity. There is little evidence that he was actually beaten up by Buckley, but it is reported that the highwayman stole 48 guineas from him.

Buckley was extremely careless after this, for he came to London and was seen there by the stock-jobber. The man quickly called for the local watch and Buckley was apprehended and taken to Newgate Prison. At his trial, the evidence of the stock-jobber ensured that Buckley was convicted of highway robbery and he was sentenced to death. This really should have been the last we hear of him, but for reasons that are not entirely clear, Buckley was reprieved. Indeed he received a pardon, for he was soon at liberty again. But Buckley being Buckley would not let the matter rest there. He was determined to have his revenge on the stock-jobber. The man had a large country house just outside the village of Hackney, and Buckley went there one night and set fire to it. But his efforts were not very successful and the fire was soon put out. There was little doubt who the culprit was and Buckley was again forced to flee.

This time he made his way to Leicestershire. He broke into a big house in Ashby-de-la-Zouch and stole £80. This enabled him to go to Derby fair and buy a good horse and he was once more in business as a highwayman. But perhaps he overestimated his own prowess, or he found that the travelers in the north were a much hardier breed than those he was used to near London. Whatever the reason, when he held up a coach only two miles from Nottingham he found he had bitten off more than he could chew. He was on his own, whereas in the coach were three gentlemen, one of them armed with a blunderbuss, and a coachmen and two servants on top. The traveler with the blunderbuss fired it though the window of the coach and killed Buckley's horse. The highwayman was thrown to the ground but he managed to grasp a pistol in each hand and, hunkering down behind his dead horse, fired on the travelers, who had now left the coach. But it was an unequal struggle. Two of the footmen were also armed and Buckley was outgunned. He managed to hit one of the gentlemen and one of the servants, both of whom later died. Buckley himself received numerous wounds and eventually became so weak from loss of blood that he was captured and taken to Nottingham gaol. This time he was not so fortunate. He was tried at the local assizes, found guilty of murder and highway robbery and hanged. His body was gibbeted at the spot where his attack on the stagecoach took place and hung there for many years. He was just twenty-nine when he died.

Isaac and Thomas Hallam, 1733

The pair who committed two of the most atrocious highway murders in the history of Lincolnshire were not born in the county at all. Isaac Hallam was born in 1709 and his brother Thomas in 1707, both near Melton Mowbray. The family moved to Lincolnshire soon after, and Isaac became a post-boy in Lincoln at the age of twelve. Since the early 1500s, the delivery of the king's dispatches (Royal Mail) had been done by riders on horseback, carrying mail between stages (or posts). The usual distance between posts was 20 miles, the distance a horse could reasonably cover before it was replaced. Each post-master was supposed to keep at least three horses and riders ready to take over the next stage. The riders were the post-boys and it was a difficult and dangerous job. They had to ride in all weathers over difficult terrain; roads – if there were any – were not paved and became muddy and almost impassable in winter. In addition they were at the mercy of highwaymen and footpads. Later, as the volume of mail increased, the post-boys were supplied with chaises – small, open two-wheeled carriages, pulled by one horse – and later still by coaches.

Isaac served diligently for five years and then went into service with Squire Pelham and then with Colonel Russell, who lived in London. When he was about twenty-one, Isaac returned to Lincoln and got his old job as a post-boy back. He also got married, but this did not seem to settle his restless spirit. He got into bad company and began frequenting alehouses and gambling dens. Soon he was in debt. The postmaster, Mr Rands, helped him out with loans, but Isaac did not seem to want to change his ways and Mr Rands got fed up with him and, determined to teach his young employee a lesson, he had him imprisoned for debt.

Being imprisoned for debt was a serious situation. Because he was imprisoned, the convict could not earn any money and thus could not repay the debt, and if he didn't get outside help he might remain in prison for years. Isaac remained in prison for five months, until Mr Rands took pity on him, revoked the debt and he was released. But smoldering resentment overtook Isaac. He gave up his job with the Post Office and moved to London to join his brother Thomas, who lived there. Together they set up in business in a brandy shop. But the business failed and they found themselves in debt. Before their creditors could have them imprisoned they absconded, and Isaac persuaded his older brother to go into the highway robbery business. Together they bought some pistols and cutlasses, and set out on 12 November 1732 on their nefarious profession.

Between then and when they were finally arrested in February 1733 they carried out fifty robberies. Mostly they haunted the roads on foot, but sometimes, when they were able to steal horses, they became more like the public's idea of a highwayman, holding up coaches in the traditional manner. Their robberies included those at Leicester, Grantham, Sleaford, Uppingham, Stamford, Northampton, Fenny Stratford, Maidenhead, Windsor, Farnham, Bagshot, Epping Forest, Grantham and Ancaster.

On Tuesday, 2 January 1733, they were about seven miles north of Ancaster when they spotted a lone horseman, a certain Thomas Matkins of Sleaford. They were able to ambush him, rob him and they took his horse. Since they only had one horse between them they both mounted the poor animal, riding north towards Lincoln. They crossed the River Witham at Washingborough Ferry, just outside Lincoln, and were going on towards Dunholme when they came upon William Wright, who was eighteen and came from Market Rasen. He was driving a chaise and he had been down to Ancaster to take a Mr Thomson, but was now on his way back to Market Rasen. He had a spare horse tethered behind the chaise and, seeing the two brothers riding one horse, he generously offered one a ride on his spare horse. This the brothers accepted with alacrity. Wright was glad of the company, since it was a long journey down to Ancaster and back, and he was even more pleased when the two rogues offered to buy him a drink in Dunholme. They stopped at the Leather Bottle public house and the brothers began plying the young man with drink. He did not known that they were desperate criminals, but they realised that the two horses that Wright had would suit them admirably and they could leave the tired horse they'd stolen from Thomas Matkins behind.

The village of Dunholme.

Old pub in Dunholme.

But Wright turned out to be more resistant to the alcohol than they had hoped and when they had left the pub and Thomas made a clumsy attempt to attack the youth he escaped into the darkness. But he couldn't travel very quickly with his chaise and two horses and the two desperadoes caught up with him near Faldingworth. They forced the chaise to stop and attacked the young man. Isaac cut his throat and they left him sitting upright in his chaise. Then, with their new horses, they turned and made their way south, passing through Linwood and on to Holton cum Beckering, where they arrived at an inn about midnight. They left the next day at about one o'clock and rode on to Lincoln. Isaac called in to see the postmaster, his old employer Mr Rands, but a row developed between the two and Isaac left in a furious temper.

The two brothers laid in wait just outside Lincoln on the road to Langworth, hoping that the postmaster himself would come through with the post. But it was a post-boy, Thomas Gardiner, who rode up at about six o'clock that night. The brothers appeared on their horses, held him up and robbed

The village of Holton cum Beckering.

him of the post. But even though it was dark the boy recognised Isaac, so Isaac cut his throat as well. Then, in a useless act
of savagery, he cut the throat of the horse. It was a stupid act
of revenge, since they could have sold the horse. They then
waited a while but the postmaster did not turn up, so they
made their way back to Lincoln to spend the night.

After that they left Lincolnshire, fearing that after two brutal
murders there would be a hue and cry for them, and made their
way to London, arriving there in the later part of January 1733.
They continued their operations, passing through Hampshire
and on to Salisbury. But they were becoming hunted men.
A reward of £40 was offered in the *London Gazette* for information that would lead to their capture. At Fisherton in
Wiltshire they robbed a man who followed them into the next
town, Wilton, where he called the watch out and the two were
captured. They were taken back to Lincolnshire, being lodged
in the George Hotel in Stamford overnight, where they were
interviewed by a reporter from the *Stamford Mercury*.

The village of Langworth.

Georgian prison in Lincoln Castle.

The village of Faldingworth.

They were tried at Lincoln Assizes in March 1733. It is reported that while he was lodged in the prison at Lincoln Castle, Isaac made an attempt to escape from his irons by filing a serrated edge to a knife the better to file through the iron manacles. But his attempt to escape was foiled. They were both convicted of murder and sentenced to death. The places of execution were chosen as the spots where they had committed the murders. Isaac was executed at a spot near Nettleham, where the post-boy was buried, and Thomas was taken to Faldingworth, where William Wright had been murdered. Both bodies were hung in chains after they were executed and, even today, a spot a mile or so north of Faldingworth is still called Gibbet Hill, where Thomas Hallam was hung.

Dick Turpin –
The Lincolnshire Connection, 1739

No chapter on highwaymen would be complete without a mention of the most famous one of all, Dick Turpin. And he did actually have a connection with Lincolnshire.

Dick Turpin was born in the village of Hempstead in Essex in 1705. His father, John Turpin, was the proprietor of the Blue Bell Inn in the village. Dick was brought up in the village and was apprenticed to a butcher, later having his own business. But he kept his prices low by stealing sheep at night and slaughtering them on his own premises. He later became a fence for a gang of thieves, the Essex Gang, who specialised in stealing deer. But they moved away from poaching into robbery, raiding the homes of wealthy merchants. At Loughton in Essex they threatened to put an elderly widow across a kitchen fire if she did not tell them where her money was. Luckily, her son intervened and told them himself. Later, when Turpin became a regular member of the gang and moved to London, they repeated the atrocity with an old farmer of Edgware. This time he was placed on the fire and one of his maidservants

A highway robbery.

was raped by one of the gang. But the authorities were on the track of the thieves and by 1735 most the gang had been broken up and hanged.

Dick Turpin was not caught and became a highwayman, regularly raiding the stagecoach from Norwich to London near his old home of Hempstead. After many adventures things were becoming too hot for him in the Essex and north London areas and he went north, first to Cambridge and then to Lincolnshire.

He settled in Long Sutton, renting rooms at the Bull Hotel under the name of Richard Palmer and giving out that he was a horse trader – the horses he traded having come from farms he raided during the night. However, he seems to have been accepted for a time in Long Sutton as a wealthy and respected citizen. He indulged in the common practice of the time of cock fighting and was also known as a gambler. It was while he was living at Long Sutton that he made one of his infrequent visits to his family in Hempstead. They knew that he was, by this time, one of the most wanted men in England, with a price on his head, but they never gave him away. It was on this visit that Turpin presented his father with the gift of a horse. When he had gone back to Lincolnshire, however, a local constable in Hempstead saw John Turpin's horse and recognised it as having been reported stolen. Turpin had in fact stolen the horse at Pinchbeck on his way down to see his father. Because John Turpin refused to say how he had come by the horse, he was arrested and held in Chelmsford Prison.

Things were not going too well for Dick Turpin in Long Sutton either. He was accused of sheep stealing, but when the local constable came to arrest him, Turpin knocked him down and made his escape. He then rode north again; stealing a horse from a convenient farm when the one he was riding became tired and in this way kept well ahead of his pursuers. He crossed the River Humber by ferry and settled in Brough. He stayed at the Ferry Inn under the name of Richard Palmer again and gave out that he was a dealer of horses. Then he moved on to Welton and established himself there. He seems to have settled down there and was accepted by the local gentry, with whom he hunted and went out shooting.

But it all went wrong one day in October 1738. Returning from a day's shooting, he noticed a chicken out in the street. It belonged to the landlord of the Cock Inn where Turpin was staying. He drew out his pistol and shot the bird. This upset the friend he was with, who remonstrated with him. But instead of apologising Turpin took umbrage and threatened to shoot the man. But his friend wasn't a person to be threatened lightly. He went to see the local magistrate to complain. When questioned, Turpin was again abusive and was taken before magistrates at Beverley. Here he was unable to call witnesses to give assurances to his good behaviour, since nobody really knew anything about him, and he was remanded in custody while enquiries were made about him. His suspected sheep stealing at Long Sutton was soon discovered, as was the fact that he'd stolen several horses in Lincolnshire. Since this was a serious crime, he was taken to York.

While he was in prison in York he wrote to his brother-in-law, who, with Turpin's father still in prison, was looking after the inn for him. But his brother-in-law said he did not know anyone in York and the letter was returned to the post office in Hempstead. It just so happened that James Smith, who had taught Turpin to write when he was at school, was in the post office when the letter came back and he recognised the handwriting. The letter was opened. Everyone knew who the son of John Turpin was and James Smith reported the facts to the authorities. He also travelled to York and identified Richard Palmer as Dick Turpin and for this he received the reward of £200 (about £27,000 in today's money).

Dick Turpin in his cave in Epping Forest.

With Dick Turpin's real identity now revealed it caused a national sensation and the papers were full of the news that the most famous highwayman in the country was now in custody. Witnesses to Turpin's earlier crimes now came forward and the evidence piled up against him. The trial at York Assizes took place on 22 March 1739. Turpin was found guilty of horse stealing and sentenced to death. He was executed on Saturday 7 April and his body buried in the churchyard of St George's Church, York. The church has now gone but the small cemetery remains, with Turpin's grave and headstone still in place.

Chapter Four

Smugglers

If you wake at midnight, and hear horses' feet,
Don't go drawing back the blind, or looking in the street,
Them that asks no questions isn't told a lie,
Watch the wall my darling, while the Gentlemen go by!

Five and twenty ponies
Trotting through the dark
Brandy for the Parson
'Baccy for the Clerk
Laces for a lady, Letters for a Spy
And watch the wall my darling, while the Gentlemen go by!

A little cottage lay among the sand dunes at the sea end of Crook Bank, to the north of Mablethorpe. One night, young Kitty and her mother were sitting by the fire when they heard a noise outside. Suddenly a sword was pushed through the window and the curtain and a loud voice shouted, 'Come out you smugglers!'

Kitty's mother shrank back in fear, but Kitty was made of sterner stuff. She went to the door, opened it and stepped outside, drawing the door closed behind her.

'Ah,' she said peering into the gloom. 'I see it's Mr Gallakin, the Customs man. What are you making all that noise about?'

The tall young man in uniform peered back at Kitty. 'Well, I didn't expect to see you here, Kitty.'

'Why ever not? It's where I live.'

'Yes, well I must have forgotten.' The young man was plainly embarrassed and because of this he gabbled on. 'You see, I was in the Tom and Jerry and I saw some lads in a corner. They were muttering among themselves and didn't notice me, so I crept up close and heard them say something about getting some stuff off the beach. And I thought Ah! Ah! I know what you all are up to. So I followed them and I'm sure they came this way.'

Kitty shook her head decisively. 'No lads came this way, or I would have heard them. But if you want to go and have a look on the beach, you're welcome. Why, it's a nice calm night and I might fancy a stroll myself.'

'You would?' said Gallakin eagerly. Then he pulled himself up. 'Of course, I shall be on duty, but on the other hand there's no reason why a lady shouldn't accompany me.' He held out his arm and Kitty took it and they strolled through the dunes to the beach.

Whether they exchanged a kiss or two afterwards we don't know, but Kitty did manage to delay Gallakin so that her father and brother and several other men could finish unloading the contraband in the sand cave at the back of the cottage.

***

Smuggling went on in Lincolnshire from the earliest times but it was very poorly documented. One of the earliest references was to smuggling in reverse. In the twelfth and thirteenth centuries Lincolnshire was one of the centres of the wool trade in this country and a great deal was exported to the Continent. But in 1274, a dispute between King Edward I and the Countess of Flanders led to an embargo on wool exports. William de Len, a Saltfleetby ship owner, together with certain merchants of Louth, sold 200 sacks of wool to the merchants of Flanders.

Saltfleet Haven.

The wool was secretly shipped aboard vessels in Saltfleet Haven and Grainsthorpe Haven and carried across to the Continent. A small amount of wool was also smuggled out via Grimsby. In 1454, Stephen Jonson of the *James* from Hull attempted to smuggle fifty-one sacks of wool and fleeces out of Grimsby, but his vessel was boarded by Customs officials after a violent fight, and his cargo confiscated. He finished up in gaol.

In 1672, the export of wool was again banned and smuggling continued out of Lincolnshire to the Continent. The coast of Lincolnshire was ideal for smuggling, with its sandy beaches and creeks and havens, and around Mablethorpe the 50ft sand dunes sheltered the beach, and from their tops it was easy to spot the coastguards and the revenue men. Farm carts could be trundled along the beach and out into the sea. Boats of shallow draught could then come in close and merchandise transferred from the carts to the boats or vice versa, and on nights when the sea was calm, tons of material could

Sand dunes to the north of Mablethorpe.

be transferred in this way. The smugglers were called 'owlers', since they worked at night. But it wasn't only the North Sea coast of Lincolnshire that could be used. It is reported that in 1785, 90 tons of wool were loaded on to a ship in Goxhill Haven in the Humber River, bound for the Continent. But soon after this the reverse smuggling of wool began to suffer a decline. The penalties for those caught doing it were severe and included hanging for the more serious offences and transportation for the less serious ones. But plenty of smuggling in the county still went on.

Taxation

Prime Minister William Pitt introduced income tax in 1799, but before that, successive governments had to raise money by taxing imports such as Dutch gin, French brandy, tobacco and tea. The taxes depended largely on how many wars the government was engaged in. At the same time there were insufficient funds to pay for ships to patrol the coastline and men to keep an eye on the coast from the land. The result was a fluctuation of smuggling, depending on the rate of the Customs. In the 1740s, the duty on tea was 4 shillings per lb (equivalent to £24 today). The annual consumption was estimated to be 1½ million lbs, but the duty collected was only on 650,000lbs: an enormous loss to the government, but a rich incentive for smugglers. And with the outbreak of war against the American Colonists in 1776, duties went up sky high as the government tried to increase its finances.

The government's way of collecting taxes was by the officers of the Board of Customs and the Board of Excise. In the eighteenth century these were two separate departments. The Customs officers were based at the major ports and had the job of boarding and searching all incoming vessels and levying the Customs duties – and they had a number of officials to help them. Of course, many incoming ships preferred to land their merchandises on secluded beaches and creeks, and it was the job of so-called Customs Riding officers to prevent this. These were usually local men with knowledge of the coast on which they were based. They were usually housed in coastal villages and it was their job to seize contraband when it came ashore. It was an extremely difficult and dangerous task. They were universally hated by the communities in which they lived, since it was their job to curtail the incomes of the smugglers, most of whom lived in those same communities. Many of the officers suffered abuse, certainly verbal and often physical as well, and it was not unknown for them to be murdered. There was often a great temptation for them to ignore what was obviously going on under their noses, or to take backhanders to turn away when operations were going on. But the Riding officers were not entirely alone. They could call upon the services of troops, cavalry from the Light Dragoon regi-

Alford market place.

ments, which were stationed in inns and public houses in the coastal villages. Mounted on speedy horses and armed with cutlasses and sabres, they could be a formidable force against the smuggling gangs and were rightly feared.

The Excise officers were responsible for collecting both taxes on imported and on home-produced goods and were therefore more widely spread than the Customs officers. They could be based in towns away from the coast. Thomas Paine, author of the *Rights of Man*, was an Exciseman and was stationed in Alford in the 1760s, but he was subsequently dismissed for misconduct. The Excise department did have officers stationed in ports, and there was often competition between the two departments.

Smuggling in the Humber

Captain Cockburn was a notable smuggler in the eighteenth century. He would load up his ship with brandy and other commodities at Dunkirk. This port, on the northern coast of

France, was a centre for smuggling. Its quays would be lined with half-anker barrels (each barrel contained 4.17 imperial gallons) of brandy or wine, and smugglers' vessels would line up outside to enter the port. The smuggling captains became so rich that many of them owned houses in Dunkirk. Captain Cockburn would take his cargo on board in Dunkirk and unload his vessel in the Humber under cover of darkness on to a Humber keel. The smaller vessel would then carry the contraband up the River Trent to Gainsborough, where it would be sold or distributed to various centres for dispersal.

Another prolific smuggler was Thomas Lumley, who was a businessman rather than a sailor. Through much of his smuggling career he lived in Grimsby; he had been a grocer, a tallow-chandler and a nail manufacturer. His preferred method of disposing of the contraband was to store it in a barn at Stallingborough. Then it was transferred to the tower at Aylesby church. He is also credited with landing Dutch gin, sometimes called Geneva, at Dent's Creek on the Humber. In fact, the practice became so common that the place received the name of New Holland, which it still has. But it all had to come to an end eventually and in 1826 Lumley was fined £1,500 (equivalent to £360,000 today) by the government.

Revenue cutters often brought smugglers' vessels which they had captured into the port of Grimsby. In 1822, the cutter *Stag* chased the vessel *Agnes* of Flushing off Whitby and finally caught and boarded the vessel and brought her into Grimsby. The smuggling vessel had a crew of twenty-five and carried 1,500 barrels of gin. A few years later, the cutter *Greyhound* captured the *Tartar of Nieuport* with 700 barrels of gin and a quantity of tobacco on board. In 1832, a veteran smuggler was captured and his ship taken to Grimsby, where it was found to contain three tons of tobacco. He was imprisoned in Lincoln Castle.

The transport of contraband from the coast to towns where it could be sold was always a problem for smugglers.

But local farmers helpfully leant their carts or themselves, ostensibly carrying goods to market with smuggled goods carefully concealed underneath the farm produce. It was risky travelling by night, because Revenue men would be suspicious of carts travelling in the darkness, and it was difficult to silence cart wheels or the hooves of horses. A story is related of a light cart carrying smuggled goods, which was travelling at night and hailed by a Customs man. The driver refused to stop and whipped up his horse. The Customs man fired and the driver fell to the ground. The official then rushed off to report and get assistance, but when he and his colleagues returned the cart and the man where nowhere to be found. The shot had missed!

Smuggling on the East Coast of Lincolnshire

The main areas of smuggling on the east coast were from Tetney Haven down to Wainfleet Haven. In the early part of the nineteenth century, tobacco was the most common commodity smuggled on this coastline. A large quantity of cigars was found concealed in a haystack on a farm near Boston, but by and large they were considered too fragile for easy transportation. Unmanufactured tobacco was easier to handle and was usually packed into hogshead barrels or in bales of 50 to 100lbs, and transferred to manufactories in Louth or Lincoln. In 1830, 600lbs of pipe tobacco, which had been captured by the Excise men, was auctioned at Louth.

In January 1843, Superintendent Campbell of Louth, together with constables Ryall and Chapman, surprised a certain John Wright of Gayton le Marsh, who was driving a cart along the Spilsby Road near Louth. They found 700lbs of leaf tobacco in the cart and he was subsequently taken before the Louth magistrates. A couple of years later a ton and a quarter of tobacco leaf was discovered in a shed

Wainfleet Haven.

belonging to a Mr Ward of Willoughby, near Alford. Mr Ward was described in the *Lincoln, Stamford and Rutland Mercury* as a 'Higgler', which means a huckster, or a man who sells small objects in the streets.

On a Sunday night in November 1833, the Customs officer stationed at Ingoldmells and accompanied by the Lloyds agent Mr James Smith of Wainfleet, boarded a smuggling vessel of some 60 tons, which was tossing in the surf. It had been run ashore by the French crew, being unfamiliar with the coast. Most of the cargo had already been spirited away, but the Customs officers were able to collect some contraband, and a search of nearby pubs soon turned up four Frenchmen, who had probably been part of the crew.

Ingoldmells was a favourite place for smugglers to land their contraband. Near there lived James White, a notorious smuggler, in a house called Leila's Cottage. He had been caught many times and had been such a persistent thorn in the side of the Customs officers that they sawed three of his boats in half.

Ingoldmells Creek.

Another well-known smuggler in the area was Joseph Lowe, who was proprietor of the Scabbed Lamb Inn. In 1834, he had been fined £1,000 for smuggling – a huge sum equivalent to £72,000 today.

On another Sunday in February 1824, the revenue cutter *Redbreast*, commanded by Lieutenant Butcher, seized a vessel near Wainfleet Haven. Most of the crew managed to escape but three were captured and the cargo – 165 barrels of gin, twenty-nine bales of tobacco, two boxes of cigars and one box of playing cards – was captured intact. The latter usually came from France and the duty on them was 2s and 6 pence (equivalent to £18 today) on each pack of cards. Later in the same year, Lieutenant Butcher repeated his success. This time most of the crew were gaoled in Lincoln Castle, but one said he was not a smuggler, but a horse dealer who had taken some horses from the Horncastle Fair over to Holland to sell them. He claimed that he was only a passenger, but was remanded until he could produce proof of his tale. The cargo was the usual gin and tobacco but it is reported that there were also some pictures and china, which the *Lincoln, Stamford and Rutland Mercury* newspaper speculated could have been 'stolen art treasures of a fallen regime'.

Further north, up the coast near Sutton-on-Sea (in those days called Sutton in the Marsh), on a bitter winter's day in 1828, some smugglers coming ashore in a 30ft boat got stuck in the ice near the shore. They were spotted by some local Customs men and the crew decided to abandon their boat in the interests of safety, so they rapidly departed, leaving the contraband – a mixture of Holland gin and tobacco – to the Customs men. The officers brought in some carts and loaded the seized merchandise on to them. The area around Sutton has high sand dunes behind the beaches, but there are lower regions in the hills called 'pullovers', because it is where carts have to be pulled over. It was on one of these, near a pub called the Ship and Cross Keys Inn, on the steep and slippery slope that the cart tipped over, scattering the cargo over the sand. It wasn't surprising, therefore, that during the resulting mêlée several barrels mysteriously disappeared.

It was in this area that a young man called George from Sutton began his smuggling career. He went with a party of older men to Holland to fetch a cargo of tobacco. On their way back they were chased by a Revenue cutter when they got near the Lincolnshire shore and had to throw the contraband overboard to lighten the ship and to plead ignorance if they were caught. But he and his colleagues persisted with later runs and were able to land cargoes at Huttoft and Mumby Chapel, both south of Sutton. In August 1850, they were caught in a gale on their way across the North Sea and had to heave-to to ride out the storm. When the wind dropped they were able to proceed and fetched up off Skegness. But mist came down and they could not see the signal from the coast. They put further out to sea to wait for the mist to clear and ran into a Revenue cutter. But they were able to make their escape in the mist

'Pullover' on Mablethorpe sand dunes.

and made their way down towards Boston. But again they ran into a Revenue cutter, this time from Wainfleet, which fired on them and ordered them to stop. The mist was now clearing and they had no hope of escape, so their only course was to dump their cargo overboard.

It might seem from the foregoing incidents that smuggling on the Lincolnshire coast was a very dangerous business and the men who tried it were nearly always caught, but this is not true. The only cases reported were those in which the smugglers were captured or thwarted. The successful smuggling operations went undetected and thus unreported, and a great deal of smuggling went on in the sixteenth, seventeenth and eighteenth centuries. Two farmer smugglers lived in the Mablethorpe area: Edward Bell, who lived at Bleak House Farm, and William Twigg, who lived at North End Farm. Both were very successful smugglers, and their farmhouses and barns – and even haystacks – were used to store contraband, before it could be taken away in farm carts. The local population ably assisted both in the landing and the storing of smuggled cargoes in chimney recesses, roof cavities and hollow haystacks, and of course they were suitably recompensed. A common saying of the time was 'put a guinea in both my eyes and I shall see nothing'. So really all we have about the smugglers and the smuggling which went on are folktales handed down from generation to generation.

Many years ago the Mablethorpe beaches became popular with Victorian society. Alfred Lord Tennyson's family would often holiday in this area when the famous poet was a young boy. Bathing huts lined the strand so that ladies could preserve their modesty by getting changed in them and stepping out into the sea. But at night, when the holidaymakers were in their beds, those same bathing huts would be used to store contraband. Many years later some schoolboys playing on the beach discovered a hogshead barrel buried in the sand, left over, no doubt, by smugglers who buried it on the beach intending to collect it later.

Mablethorpe smugglers were adept at 'foxing', which was luring coastguards away from an intended landing area by placing lights in appropriate positions, or dropping hints in pubs that a boat would be coming ashore at a certain place, when in fact it would coming ashore at a different one. It was possible sometimes to treat Customs officers if they were found in pubs and they were often amenable to having free drinks with the locals. In one case the officer received so many free drinks that he became boastful and claimed that he could catch any smuggler 'even though he should jump over a gout first' (a 'gout' is a dyke). When asked to prove this, he took the locals out to a suitable gout and offered to jump it. Of course in his present condition he failed and fell into the water. When he had gone home to change into dry clothes the locals got on with the job of landing a cargo on the beach.

Another Mablethorpe resident tells of a time when she was a little girl. Mary West's father was a smuggler, and one night his ship was spotted and chased by a Revenue cutter. The Customs men fired on the smugglers' vessel and one of the seamen was injured. The vessel eventually made her escape and the injured sailor was brought ashore and put to bed in Mary's father's house. Mary knew nothing of this, having been in bed asleep at the time. But she was woken during the night by groans coming from a nearby room. She lay terrified expecting a ghost to walk in, but nothing happened, though the groaning continued. Eventually she plucked up the courage to get out of bed and creep out on to the landing. The groans were coming from the spare room and she peeped inside, to be terrified again when she saw a strange man's head peering at her over the bedclothes. The next morning the local doctor turned up. He asked no questions and a few days later the sailor was well enough to go home. The doctor subsequently found a keg of brandy on his doorstep.

Innkeepers were often involved in smuggling, particularly spirits. One near Mablethorpe also had customs officials billeted on him. He kept on good terms with them by frequently treating them with wine and spirits, which were part of his smuggled horde, while he entertained his smuggling colleagues in another part of the inn. He had a special friend, the only name being handed down being that of Billy, who used to supply him with spirits smuggled over from Holland in a small open boat. This hazardous operation brought Billy a comfortable living, except on one night, when he and a friend who had come with him were unloading contraband on the shore. They had already unloaded some and gone back to the boat for more when a Riding officer discovered the pile of goods on the beach. Not realising the smugglers were nearby he fired his pistol to summon assistance. Billy and his friend heard the shot and hurriedly made off in the boat into the darkness. But Billy risked his neck once too often. On one of his trips from Holland he disappeared and was never seen again.

A story is told of a Riding officer who one night, while out on his rounds, accidentally rode into a large pit in the darkness.

He shouted for assistance and some people living nearby heard him and, with great difficulty, got him and his horse out of the pit. Nearby, however, there was a fair-sized stream, which led up into the Wolds. While the officer was being hauled out of the pit, smugglers loaded up a small craft and paddled upstream under the cover of the commotion going on some distance away. Several of these streams finish up near chalk quarries on the edge of the Wolds, where the contraband could be hidden. Today, there are still several disused chalk quarries to the south of Louth. Around Little Cawthorpe there are four within a mile of each other. It was afterwards suggested that the Riding officer's fall into the pit was staged between the Customs officer and the smugglers to draw attention away from the smuggling operation. The officer, no doubt, was suitably recompensed.

Smuggling in Modern Times

Although the following story is not strictly modern, it shows that nothing much has changed in the smuggling business. A case came before the Boston magistrates on Tuesday, 22 August 1922. When a German ship, the *Albert Sauber*, came into port, Stanley Jones, the Waterguard officer, went on board and asked the crew to sign the usual declaration that there was no contraband on the vessel. But he was suspicious of one of the crew, Reinheld Strehl, and asked him personally if he had anything to declare. The seaman produced two ounces of shag tobacco. The Waterguard officer asked him if he had any sprits or drugs and Strehl said no. But the officer was not satisfied. They had had trouble with this vessel before and had found concealed spirits on her, so he decided that he would make a search again, and, in the forecastle, he found two bottles of brandy concealed in an empty stove. It may not sound much today, but at that time there was no Common Market and regulations against the importation of spirits were very strict. Reinheld Strehl was fined £2 14s 9d, with 7s 6d costs (equivalent to £110 and £15.20 today) or a month in prison if he couldn't pay. Reinheld said that his ship had sailed and he had no money. He would have to write to his sweetheart in Germany for the money – he was remanded into custody.

Today, even with the lifting of restrictions on trade by the European Common Market, smuggling is still rife. Drugs, guns and illegal aliens are still being brought into the ports of Immingham, Grimsby and Boston and sometimes flown in to small airports. Then you have the luxury trade of diamonds, gold, watches, art (artworks usually stolen from galleries and stately homes) and of course cigarettes and spirits. And in an echo of the past, HM Customs, Humberside Police and Immigration officials recently announced a tightening of the patrols on the River Humber to combat illegal activities occuring on the river.

Chapter Five

Fraud

Forgery

Forgery must be one of the oldest of misdemeanours, and almost all classes of people have resorted to it at times. A most interesting case concerns the monks of Crowland Abbey. Sometimes called Croyland Abbey, it exists today as a Church of England parish church, which is all that is left of the extensive abbey it once was. Crowland Abbey, some sixteen miles from Stamford and thirteen miles from Peterborough, lies deep in the Fens close to the River Welland. This was no accident, since, in earlier times, there were few roads and many relied on the river for transport. The Fens, before they were drained in the late eighteenth and early nineteenth century, and particularly during the winter, were a waste of water with a few islands dotted about on which human habitation could occur. Between AD 699 and AD 714, a monk named Guthlac came to live as a hermit on one of these islands. He was eventually followed by a monastic community later on in the eighth century. An abbey was founded and it became one of the earliest of the Anglo-Saxon monasteries in Lincolnshire. It was sacked sev-

The parish church of Crowland and the west front of the ruined nave of Crowland Abbey. (Courtesy Thorvaldsson)

eral times by the Danes, but afterwards rebuilt, and, because of its relative remoteness, it avoided being involved in many of the upheavals which the rest of the country suffered. It became one of the wealthiest of the East Anglian abbeys, and noble visitors frequented it to pay tribute to the shrine of St Guthlac.

Monasteries and abbeys from the earliest times were regarded as places of solace and godliness, but with their increasing wealth came corruption; moral standards decayed and many were regarded with suspicion and hostility by local people. The Abbey of Crowland owned a great deal of land, over which the monks grazed sheep and cattle, and the abbey had substantial fishing rights in the rivers and streams around it. All this earned the monks enmity from the local population, who in times of bad harvest would frequently go hungry while the wealthy monks, of whom there would be no more than forty in residence at any one time, feasted on the best quality food and wine.

In the late fourteenth and early fifteenth centuries, the abbey was involved in a number of disputes with local people. Men from Market Deeping and Deeping St James invaded the abbey territory, and the abbot had to go to London and petition the King for restitution. This resulted in the Deeping men being imprisoned in Lincoln Castle. Later on, villagers from Moulton and Weston occupied an island on the abbey territory and fished in waters, which were strictly for abbey use

The village of Market Deeping.

only. They were joined by men from Spalding, who also fished in the disputed areas and destroyed the abbey's fishing nets. The abbot by this time had become blind and his prior took over the dispute. He first received permission from the Bishop of Lincoln to excommunicate the invaders and then he went to London to have the matter thrashed out in court.

He was able to produce documents that proved that the land the abbey had been granted had been agreed to by the Saxon kings, Ethelbald, Edred and Edgar. At about the same time, a history of Crowland Abbey was produced by the monks, which incorporated many of the charters supposedly given by the Saxon kings, but also gave a detailed picture of monastic life. The documents and the history were accepted by the courts and the monks of Crowland won their case.

These documents became an essential document for historical research and continued to be used by scholars up until the end of the eighteenth century. But by the nineteenth century, scholars were beginning to wonder about it. It referred to people and places in language appropriate to the fourteenth century, which would have been different in the tenth century, when it was supposedly written. It also referred to monks who had studied at Oxford University *before* the university was founded. And it also referred to a triangular bridge in the tenth century, when such bridges were not invented until the fourteenth. But most bizarrely, when the birth and death dates were gone into more closely, it was apparent that some of the monks had supposedly lived to incredible ages: 115, 142 and even 148 were calculated. Most historians decided that the history was a forgery, but it must be admitted that it was one of the most successful forgeries ever perpetrated. It didn't do Crowland Abbey much good, however, for a hundred years later Henry VIII brought in the dissolution of the abbeys and monasteries. The Abbot of Crowland Abbey sent a present of fish, from the Fens, to Cromwell, who was overseeing the Dissolution, but it did no good. The abbey was dissolved in 1539.

William Dodd (1729-1777)

William Dodd was the eldest son of the vicar of Bourne
and was born in that town on 29 May 1729. He was a clever
child and did well at school and went on to Clare College,
Cambridge at the age of sixteen. There he took his degree with
first class honours and was admitted to the list of Wranglers
(those students who obtained first class honours in mathemat-
ics). In those days there was not much call for mathematicians,
so young Dodd decided to try his luck as an author. He left
university without taking any more degrees and moved to
the metropolis. But this young man, with a brilliant academic
future before him, soon became seduced by the glamour and
excitement of London highlife. His living became extrava-
gant and he rapidly fell into debt. He might have salvaged his
position by marrying a wealthy woman, since he was good
looking with a pleasing manner. But he fell in love with a
domestic servant, who had little money of her own, and married her. This only added to his expenses, but he seemed loath
to change his way of life. He rented and furnished on credit a
large expensive house in Wardour Street.

Luckily, his friends could see the difficultly he was getting
himself into and appealed to his father. The vicar came to town,
paid his son's debts and advised him to give up the house, which
he did. He also set his son on a more productive path and young
Dodd was ordained a deacon soon after. He became a curate at
West Ham and, to supplement his small income, superintended
the education of a few young gentlemen. He also continued
with his studies and received the degrees of Master of Arts and
later Doctor of Laws at Cambridge, as well as becoming a chaplain to the King. One of Dodd's pupils was the eldest son of
Lord Chesterfield and when his father died in 1773 and he succeeded to the peerage, he appointed Dr Dodd as his chaplain.

But Dodd continued with his expensive habits and when he
failed to obtain the Rectory of West Ham, when the incum-

bent died, which would have increased his salary, he moved out. He obtained the Rectory of Hockcliffe in Bedfordshire. This still did not provide him with sufficient income for his purposes, and when Bishop Moss received the see of Bath and Wells, and the valuable Rectory of St George, in Hanover Square, became vacant, Dodd felt that this would suit him admirably. It was in the royal prerogative to grant this and, desperate to obtain the living, he wrote a letter to Lady Apsley, one of Her Majesty's ladies-in-waiting, offering her £3,000 if she could help to arrange this. Lady Apsley was appalled. She immediately showed the letter to the Lord Chancellor. Dodd had not signed the letter, but it was easily traced back to him and his name was ordered to be struck off the list of chaplains to the King. But this was nothing to the opprobrium he received in the press.

Dodd fled to Geneva and stayed there with an influential old pupil of his, who took pity on him and offered him the Rectory of Wringe in Buckinghamshire. Later in the year he moved back to England, but he refused to curtail his high life and continued to spend money he didn't have. At this stage another scheme presented itself to him, whereby he could obtain money by underhand means. This time he would forge the signature of another of his ex-pupils, the Earl of Chesterfield. He pretended that the Earl urgently wanted to borrow £4,000, but that he wanted to do this secretly. Dodd employed a go-between, Lewis Robertson, to act for him. Robertson presented a bond not signed, but for the amount in question, to various money lenders, telling them it was for a young noble lord who wished to remain anonymous. Not surprisingly he didn't get many takers, but eventually found a firm, Fletcher & Peach, who agreed to advance the money. Robertson then gave the bond to Dodd for signature. It was returned the next day with the signature of the Earl of Chesterfield upon it and Robertson received his £4,000, which he passed on to Dodd.

He would have got away with it too, but for an unfortunate accident. A clerk in the offices of Fletcher & Peach spilled some ink on the document and it was decided to rewrite it. Naturally enough they passed the document to the Earl and asked him if he would re-sign it. He spotted the forgery and the fat was in the fire. Dodd was arrested at his house in Argyle Street. He immediately confessed and offered to repay the money. To do this he mortgaged his house and all his property to cover the amount. But his offer was rejected. He was taken before the Lord Mayor of London and charged with forgery. His trial came up at the Old Bailey on 19 February 1777. Dodd made an impassioned plea for clemency, but the jury took only ten minutes to bring in a verdict of guilty, although they did, however, present a petition to the King for mercy. But Dodd was condemned to death, for forgery was at the time a hanging offence.

The press, which had only a short time before excoriated him, now turned in his favour. Many letters appeared asking for clemency and Samuel Johnson wrote several papers in his defence. 'The Convict's Address to his Unhappy Brethren', which Dodd used as his last sermon, was in fact written by Dr Johnson himself, as revealed in Boswell's *Life of Samuel Johnson*. But Dr Johnson never publicly admitted to the fact, insisting that Dodd had written it and quoting his famous remark, 'Depend upon it sir, when a man knows he is going to be hanged in a fortnight, it concentrates his mind wonderfully'. It is said that 23,000 people signed a petition asking for a pardon. But it was rejected and Dr William Dodd was hanged at Tyburn on 27 June 1777.

John George Haigh (1909-1949)

John George Haigh has a special place in the annals of crime. Apart from being one of the most prolific English murderers of the twentieth century (he is known to have murdered six people and possibly more), he is chiefly known for dissolving the bodies in acid – a very rare method of disposing of corpses. He is also recognised as one of the most expert forgers of his time. A fuller account of his life, including how he was finally brought to justice, is given in *Murder & Crime: Lincoln*. We shall be concerned here only with his forgeries.

Haigh was born in Stamford on 27 July 1909, but soon after, his family moved to Outwood Colliery, near Wakefield, where his father had a position as an electrical engineer. Young Haigh was a bright boy and won a scholarship to the Wakefield Cathedral Choir School and sang for some years in the choir. He was a gifted musician and in his later years often played the piano for his friends' enjoyment. He was a good artist too, which he proved by being able to forge his teachers' signatures so that they were accepted as genuine. But he was also lazy. His teachers reported that he was brilliant at what he was inter- ested in, but wouldn't bother with subjects to which he was indifferent. The result was that he left school without much in the way of qualifications. He worked first in a garage, then in a succession of other jobs, which he left or was asked to leave because he often couldn't be bothered to turn up for work. But the lure of easy money was always with him and he decided he could make more by working for himself.

By the time he was twenty-one he had started his own advertising agency and he dabbled in conveyancing and buying and selling houses. But this did not bring in enough money and he began selling cars. The only problem was that they were not his to sell. He bought cars on hire purchase by forging the documents and then sold them. This brought in a lot of money quickly and on the strength of it he got married. But it was also easily detected and the new Mrs Haigh soon found herself on her own as Haigh received fifteen months imprisonment. She didn't visit him in prison and he only saw her once when he came out.

Haigh was released in December 1935 and immediately went to London to start a new life. Pintable machines were all the rage and for a time Haigh worked for a Mr McSwan before leaving and starting up in business on his own – not as a pintable operator, but as a solicitor, using a name he picked out of the Law List. He would put an attractive advertisement in local papers saying that he was winding up an estate and was prepared to sell off shares at below market price. All he asked from people interested was a 25 per cent deposit. The money rolled in and Haigh pocketed it and moved on to another town. But when he moved to Guildford he misspelled the name of the town on his letterhead, missing out the 'd'. This led to him being traced and arrested and, at the Surrey Assizes on 24 November 1937, he received four years penal servitude.

When he came out of prison the Second World War was on and Haigh went into the pintable business himself. Mr McSwan had by now retired as a very rich man, owning several houses. His son, Donald McSwan, was worried about being called up for military service and he asked Haigh if he could help him forge some documents to keep him out of the army. But Haigh, seeing yet another way of making money, lured young Donald to his basement flat in Gloucester Road, where he killed the young man and dissolved his body in acid. He then went to Donald's parents and told them that their son had gone secretly to Glasgow, but would communicate with them through Haigh. He forged letters from their son, which apparently fooled the parents completely and they duly passed over money for their son to Haigh. But it was too good to last. Eventually the McSwans demanded their son's address, as they wanted to visit him. There was nothing for it. Haigh took them to Gloucester Road and disposed of them in the same way as their son. Now he was really in the money. He forged Donald's signature on a power of attorney and this gave him access to the four properties the McSwans owned, and, by forging transfers for the guilt-edged securities the McSwans held, he was able to secure their money. It is estimated that he netted about £4,000 in total, which was a great deal of money in those days.

Haigh moved into the Onslow Court Hotel and began living the high life, buying expensive cars and doing some heavy gambling. By August 1947 he was overdrawn at the bank. But not far away lived a promising couple. Dr Archie Henderson, a wealthy GP, and his wife Rose had just put their house up for sale. Haigh read about it and made them an offer, way above the asking price. Rose wrote to her brother that she'd just met the most stupid man she'd ever come across. Of course Haigh didn't want to buy the house, he just wanted to get to know the couple. And he did. He became quite friendly with them, taking them out for meals and trips to the theatre. He had, by this time, acquired a workshop in Crawley in Sussex and one day he offered to show Archie around it. While he was there Haigh shot him. Then he contacted Rose and told her that Archie had been taken ill and he would take her to him. He killed her there too and again dissolved the bodies in acid.

The following day he turned up at the Brighton hotel where the Hendersons had been staying with a letter of authority apparently signed by the Hendersons, paid their hotel bill and took charge of their property. He sold their car and with forged deeds got hold of their house, which he then sold. He sold off Rose's jewellery and, with the Henderson's savings, received just over £7,000. Rose used to telephone her brother regularly and Haigh told him that they had gone away because Archie had got himself in trouble. Then Rose's brother received a letter from her explaining things and saying that everything was all right. In fact, they started up a correspondence and the brother seemed quite satisfied, at least for a time.

But as always Haigh soon ran through the money and looked around for another victim. This time he foolishly selected a rich widow living in the same hotel as himself, a Mrs Durand-Deacon. He took her down to the workshop in Crawley. But, unfortunately for him, he had been seen earlier that day at the hotel with Mrs Durand-Deacon and her friend went to the police when she disappeared. The police interviewed Haigh and when they discovered his record the mystery began to unravel and he soon confessed to her murder and the murders of the Hendersons and the McSwans. This was the first time it was even recognised that they were missing.

The trial was the sensation of the day, with Hollywood film stars even coming over for the trial. Haigh was quickly convicted and was hanged in August 1949. But for his consummate skill as a forger, he might have been discovered years before and lives might have been saved.

Conmen

There are as many stories about conmen as there are conmen themselves. One sold the Eiffel Tower (twice), another Nelson's Column and several other public buildings in London. Some

The village of Tealby.

Market Rasen station.

cons were exceedingly complicated, others very simple, but the ones that succeeded did so mainly due to the greed or gullibility of the victims. I have selected just two, both with connections to Lincolnshire.

It was on a cold night in January 1856 when a stranger knocked at the door of farmer Richard Brumby, who had eighteen acres near the village of Tealby, some three miles from Market Rasen. The door was opened by his wife Sarah who, like her husband, was fifty-five years old. In the doorway stood a tall, thin man in outdoor clothes.

'I've just come off the train at Market Rasen,' he explained. He had a slightly singsong accent which the farmer's wife had never heard before. 'And I would normally be making my way to Louth – my father is an ironmonger there – but I've left a lot of luggage at the station as I've just come back from Australia – '

'Australia, did you say? Why, my eldest son has emigrated to Australia,' exclaimed Mrs Brumby.

'Yes I know. I met him out there and he's sent you some stuff – '

'Well then come on in. You can tell us all about him. You don't want to be travelling the roads to Louth tonight. It's cold and there could be snow over the Wolds. What do you say to staying the night with us? That will be all right, won't it father?'

Richard Brumby, who was sitting at the kitchen table with the rest of the family, looked a little unsure, but his youngest daughter Martha, who was sixteen, chimed in, 'Oh do let him stay father.' Richard Brumby, after some hesitation, nodded.

And so the stranger, who said his name was James Jackson, came in and a place was made for him at the table. He shared in the Brumbys' simple meal and told them all about their eldest son, who they had not heard of for a long time and said that he had sent them a nugget of gold, which was worth a lot of money, and, in addition, he had sent some dresses for his mother and also for his sister Martha. Martha was very excited to hear about this and imagined herself dressing up in the new clothes, for she didn't have a lot of clothes. James also regaled them with stories of what he called the 'Outback' and the curious animals that lived there, including the kangaroo. He kept the family enthralled until it was time to go to bed and gratefully accepted their offer of staying the night. Just before he went to bed, he told Richard Brumby that he had left some boxes at Market Rasen station, including the box containing the dresses for the Brumby ladies and the gold nugget.

'Do you think I ought to hire a trap to take my boxes with me to Louth tomorrow? You see I'm a bit short of cash, for the travelling from Australia has been very expensive.'

The farmer stood a little undecided, and then he shrugged his shoulders and went to the drawer where they kept their money. If the young man had been so kind as to bring all the presents from their son in Australia the least they could do would be to lend him some cash. He took out a cashbox and unlocked it with a key he took from his pocket. He handed some coins to James Jackson. 'That should see you all right until you get to Louth.'

Jackson thanked him profusely and said that he would drop off the box containing the family's possessions on his way to Louth the next morning. And then they all went to bed.

The next morning Richard Brumby and his two sons were up early and set off to work, as was their usual way, coming back later for breakfast. While they were having their breakfasts Sarah Brumby remarked that James Jackson had not come down yet and Richard told her to send Martha up to knock on his door. Martha did so but reported that there was no answer to her knock and when Richard investigated, he found that their visitor had gone.

'Perhaps he went down early to the station,' said Martha.

Her father shook his head. 'You'd better get down to the station yourself my girl.'

Martha raced down to the station but she could see no boxes there, and the stationmaster told her that he had seen no traveler from Australia with or without boxes. When she got back to the farmhouse the family discovered that the cashbox was missing. All this was reported in the *Lincoln Rutland and Stamford Mercury* for 25 January 1856. The paper also reported that there had been several other cases of a mysterious stranger, apparently from Australia, who had approached other farms in the area with similar stories, but without a great deal of success.

The Brumbys reported the theft to Sergeant Allbones of Market Rasen and he made energetic efforts to catch the conman, but he did not succeed. A week later the Marshal family of Ludford were also conned by the smooth-talking stranger. But the victims in Lincolnshire had to wait until the following year to hear the news they wanted. On 6 March 1857, the same newspaper reported that a James Jackson, alias Smith, had been enquiring at Sharnbrook in Bedfordshire, claiming to be a missionary from Australia, and looking for two widows who had relatives in the colony and to whom he was to give £10. The local superintendent, W.B. Graham, heard about this, went to the village and managed to catch the conman before he disappeared again. There seems to be no further information about the man calling himself James Jackson. It is quite likely that he was convicted and transported for life, probably to Australia!

Lincolnshire Lothario

'Get out! Get Out! What are you doing in my house? Get out immediately!'

The young man thus addressed did not argue, but rapidly left the house on Back Lane, Winteringham. In the 1930s it was a small village on the banks of the Humber, to the north of Scunthorpe. Mrs Hincliffe, who had demanded the young man's exit, watched him go from the front window. But he only went as far as the front garden and he was soon joined by Mrs Hincliffe's twenty-four-year-old daughter, Irene. Mrs Hincliffe had returned from a trip away and found them together. Her husband was a steamroller driver and had jobs all round the country. Mrs Hincliffe often went with him, leaving behind her daughter Irene and her son Arthur. It was from one of these trips that she had returned to find this strange young man making himself at home in her house.

When she saw her daughter join this young man in the garden she marched out of the house. 'Who are you and what were you doing in my house?' she demanded.

The young man spoke pleasantly. 'My name is Arthur Vamplew and I'm on leave from the RAF.'

But before he could say any more Irene chimed in, 'We were married at Brigg Registry Office yesterday, so there!'

This completely astounded Mrs Hincliffe and she was struck dumb for a period. But she soon rallied. 'All right, so you are married. Where's the marriage certificate?' But if she expected this to flummox the two she was wrong, for Arthur Vamplew replied quite calmly, 'I'm sorry to spring this on you Mrs Hincliffe, but we really are married. But because I'm in the RAF, to get the married man's allowance I've had to send off the certificate to my commanding officer to prove that Irene and are married.'

Mrs Hincliffe's head was spinning. The only possible reason she could think of for such a precipitate wedding was that

Irene was pregnant! And it flashed through her mind that this might result in a possible scandal in the village. What would the neighbours think? This was, after all, the 1930s, when illegitimacy and babies born suspiciously early was a cardinal sin and would result in it going round the village in no time. And what would people think of the family then?

'You'd better come inside,' she said.

Mrs Hincliffe was a philosophical woman and, in any case, there was little she could do about the situation, so she accepted young Arthur Vamplew. She took him into her family and made the best of it. But the marriage certificate seemed a long time coming and the young airman seemed to be having a very long leave, and Mrs Hincliffe became suspicious. So, one day, she went to the Registry Office in Brigg to check up on the illusive certificate. She found that they had no record of a marriage between her daughter and Arthur Vamplew.

Mrs Hincliffe was furious. Back she went to the house in Winteringham all geared up for a final showdown with the couple. But once again she was forestalled, this time by Irene herself, who cheerfully admitted that she was not married, but suggested that perhaps she ought to be.

'Well, are you pregnant or not?'

'I'm not quite sure. I might be.'

Mrs Hincliffe thought of all the times the young couple had been sleeping together in her house and saw the looming scandal. 'You'd better get married at once!' She took her reluctant charges to the church at Winteringham to book the wedding and get the bans read. She also had to lend Vamplew money to get the bans read and to buy him some new shoes for the ceremony. While he was staying at Back Lane she charged him £1 a week, but this had to go on account until his money from the RAF came through. All was set up for the wedding, which was due to take place on 7 October 1931. Mrs Hincliffe even went so far as to negotiate for them to rent a cottage in the village so they could set up home together. But the day before the wedding Mrs Hincliffe returned home from shopping to find the house empty. The pair had gone.

She was distraught. The fact that Vamplew had gone would not have upset her too much. But the fact that he had taken Irene with her upset her far more. Irene obviously wanted to be with him and so she had accompanied him. But what if he found her an encumbrance? Supposing she had a baby and he didn't want it. Would he simply abandon her, or would he do something worse? She decided to go to the police. Normally the police would have classed Irene as a missing person, but since she had apparently gone away voluntarily would not have been greatly concerned. But Mrs Hincliffe complained that Vamplew owed her money for rent and all the other things she had paid for on the promise of being repaid by the young man. Suddenly he was wanted for obtaining money by false pretences.

Poor Irene was quickly found. Two days later she was found alone and without any money and reduced to sleeping on Paddington station. She was returned to her home in Winteringham a much-chastened young lady. Apparently, Vamplew's money had come through and he had persuaded her to go away with him, saying that he had a flat in London, a job to go to and that he would marry her in the metropolis. But he simply abandoned her and left her alone and adrift in the big city.

It is easy to sympathise with Irene. In the 1930s there were few jobs open to women without good qualifications and they were further restricted by not being able to obtain a mortgage. The only solution for most young women was to get married. Irene was twenty-four, an age when most of her village contemporaries were already married, many with families of their own. And when she was introduced to the handsome, smooth-talking airman she fell for him in a big way. She claimed afterwards that he came unbidden to her home while her mother was away and would not leave, although he slept at first with her brother. Whether this is true seems doubtful.

Arthur Vamplew finally came to court in December 1931. He pleaded not guilty, but when the evidence of his appalling conduct was presented in court, his counsel forced him to change his plea, saying that if he did not plead guilty he would refuse to represent him. He went to prison for three months, but the trauma Irene suffered, when it all came out, must have been of much longer duration.

Coining

The manufacture of fake coins was a widespread crime in earlier times, even though up until the early nineteenth century the penalty was death. Various cheap metals could be cast in moulds and the coin coloured to make it look like silver. This took some expertise and few people actually did it. A couple who did were caught in Leicester in July 1783. Edward Perplar, his wife Eleanor and a William Dale had been suspected of passing fake coins in Grantham. They were followed to a lodging house in Leicester and given in charge of the local constable. Most people carried their belongings around with them when they travelled – in bundles, for suitcases were not common. The bundles of the three were examined and some fake money was discovered in them. Also found were moulds for casting metals and a pot of a material used to colour brass to make it look like silver. Usually the lower value silver coins were faked, as these were easier to pass without suspicion. The constable took the three before the Mayor of Leicester and he sent them under guard back to Grantham, where they were taken before the magistrates. They were then transferred to Lincoln Castle Prison and appeared on trial at the next assizes on 4 August. They were charged with 'feloniously colouring or casting over with some wash or other materials to produce the colour of silver, fifteen pieces of metal resembling the coins of the realm'. The two men said that Eleanor Perplar had not been involved either in the manufacture or the passing of the fake coins. This was accepted by the court and she was acquitted. The two men were not so lucky. They were both found guilty and condemned to death. On 22 August they were taken on a sledge to the place of execution and there hanged.

Later on, the crime of coining was not visited by such extreme punishments. In 1847, David Worrill tried to pass some fake shillings in Barton for tea and tobacco. The shopkeeper followed the man, in the company of a local constable, and Worrill's house was searched. A mould for casting shillings was found and he was taken to court. His rather lame excuse was that he had found the mould in a dyke, but this did not prevent him being convicted and he was sentenced to seven years transportation.

Some of the coins made as fakes were really not up to the job. A young woman called Keziah Franklin proffered a shilling when buying ale at The Bell public house in Spalding in February 1862. The man behind the bar looked at it suspiciously, and then bent it between his fingers. It was made of pewter instead of silver. Being of a kind nature he gave the coin back and asked her to give him some real money. But she put the coin back in her pocket and, leaving her ale standing on the counter, left the pub quickly. She should have stopped there, but she went straight round to the shop of John Cox and proffered the fake coin, now flattened out, and asked him if he would change it for two sixpences. John Cox was not as observant as the proprietor of The Bell and he accepted it in good faith and gave her two sixpences. Later on he had another look at the coin and realised that it was a fake. He immediately got in touch with the local constable. Then young Keziah Franklin made her second mistake. Seized perhaps with an attack of conscience she came back to the shop and offered the shopkeeper a real shilling in exchange for the fake one she had given him earlier. But it was already too late. She was marched off to the lock-up and subsequently received a sentence of a year's hard labour at the local House of Correction.

In March of the same year a William Brown tried to buy a pound of butter at the Grantham butter market with a fake florin. Unfortunately for him he was being watched, as he had been suspected of passing fake coins for goods earlier that day. He was taken in charge and the florin was found to be a fake. When he was searched, three other fake florins were found on him. He said that he had been given the coins in exchange for a knife and a neck cloth. But, unfortunately for him, he had already been convicted at Nottingham in 1856 of passing fake coins and had served a year in prison. This time he received three years.

Chapter Six

Murder

It has been said that murder is the most democratic of crimes since all classes of people commit it. Bank robbery, kidnapping and robbery are largely committed by what used to be called the criminal classes, or at least people who set themselves to operate outside the law. But murder is committed by everybody, from the lowest to the highest; even kings have resorted to murder when it suited them and you can find murderers in all trades and professions, or even no trade or profession at all. But the most intriguing and sometimes the most spectacular murders often occur in prosaic and humdrum situations. The following selection illustrates this.

Tom Otter, 1805

On the face of it this was just a rather dull, routine case of a man killing his wife, but somehow the story has become one of the most famous in the history of Lincolnshire. Tom Otter has a petrol station, a bridge and a lane named after him. How this came about was due to an unforeseen and incredible series of events which have passed into the folklore of the county.

Tom Otter wasn't even born in the county. His birthplace was Treswell, near Retford in Nottinghamshire. His mother, Ann, was fifty-one when she had him in 1778. He was the third child and his father died when Tom was sixteen and he was brought up by an uncle. His job was a 'banker', that is a labourer who worked on the banks of dykes and rivers, such as the Trent. They were regarded as rough, tough characters with little respect for the law. Otter seems to have been just such a character, but he also had a propensity for picking up and seducing young women, and even before he came to Lincoln he was reported to have a wife and child who lived in a village near Southwell, Nottinghamshire.

In 1805, Tom Otter was working on the old Swanpool in Lincoln when he met Mary Kirkham, who was twenty-four. She soon became pregnant by him and pressed him for marriage. At the time a pregnant single woman was regarded as a disgrace to the community, since she would likely be a drain on resources. She could be summoned before the magistrates, and if she didn't reveal the father she could end up in the local House of Correction. If the father was known he would be made the object of a bastardy order and would be required to pay £40 over a period to cover such things as the midwife's fee and other expenses. So, on 3 November 1805, Tom Otter found himself taken by cart by two local constables to the church at South Hykeham, there to be married to Mary Kirkham, in what we would today call a shotgun wedding. It is said that Tom stood before the priest between the two constables to make his vows. But he didn't use his real name. No doubt realising that word might get back to his first wife in Southwell, he called himself Temporel, his mother's maiden name.

But Tom was not too pleased at having been forced into the marriage and he determined to do something about it. The couple made their way back up to Lincoln and thence westwards, along what is now the A57, to the village of Saxilby.

Saxilby stands on the bank of the Fosdyke Canal and it was at The Sun Inn in the village that the two stopped for a drink at about six o'clock at night. Tom then invited his new bride to go for a walk with him and the innocent young girl followed him along the banks of the Fossdyke to a place called Drinsey Nook, just over a mile from Saxilby. There he led his wife into a field just off the road.

'Sit down Mary, you can rest here.'

When the young woman had sat down gratefully in the stubble field, Tom strode off to the hedge and, with great difficulty, pulled a large hedge stake out of the ground. He lifted it high in the air and brought it crashing down on the poor Mary's head, shouting, 'This will finish my knob-stick wedding!' He struck again and again until her skull was crushed with the blows.

Mary's body was found by two men the next morning. The inquest at The Sun Inn opened on 5 November. Tom and Mary had been recognised at the inn before their fatal walk and several people had seen them on the turnpike road before that. The hedge stake was found near the scene of the crime and produced at the inquest. The verdict of the inquest was

The Sun Inn at Saxilby.

St Botolph's Church at Saxilby.

'willful murder against her husband Thomas Temporal.' He was recognised and arrested in Lincoln soon after and taken to the prison in the castle. Mary was buried in the graveyard at St Botolph's Church in Saxilby.

The trial of Tom Otter took place at the Lincoln Assizes on 12 March 1806, before Baron Sir Robert Graham. It lasted five hours and involved twenty witnesses. Otter offered no defence and the jury brought in a verdict of guilty after only a few minutes deliberation. He was condemned to death and was hanged on the roof of Cobb Hall at the castle on 14 March. Such were the circumstances of the crime that it was felt that mere execution was not enough and the judge ordered that the body should be gibbeted. This was carried out on 20 March.

In gibbeting, the body is held inside an iron cage and suspended from the crossbeam of a post. It was hung at or near the scene of the crime, often at a crossroads, so that it would be seen by as many people as possible and act as a deterrent to those considering a life of crime. It took some time for the gibbeting to be done in Tom Otter's case, since the cage had to be especially

made by a blacksmith at Saxilby. The body then had to be covered in pitch to prevent birds pecking away at it. It was a mournful procession which crossed the bridge over the Fossdyke at Saxilby that day in March. According to legend, the bridge collapsed after the cart containing the body had passed over it. In addition, when the gibbet was being raised at a spot near Drinsey Nook, still commemorated today by Gibbet Wood which stands nearby, the high wind caused considerable difficulty and several times the whole structure collapsed, killing one of the workmen.

Convicted highwaymen were often gibbetted as a deterrent to others.

So began the legend of Tom Otter. But one of the most incredible features of the case only arose after Otter had been executed and gibbeted. A certain John Dunkerley, who was a local farm labourer, was having a few drinks in The Sun Inn at Saxilby one night in November 1805. He had rather too many as it turned out and when he came out of the pub he was really in no fit state to walk home to Doddington, three miles to the south. He staggered along the bank of the Fossdyke, being extremely lucky not to fall in, until he reached Drinsey Nook, and then cut inland towards Doddington. By this time he was so tired that he turned into a field, lay down and was soon asleep. He was awakened from his slumbers by voices and, opening one eye, saw two figures coming into the field. It turned out to be Tom Otter and his newlywed, Mary. He lay

Drinsey Nook.

there horrified while he watched Tom tell Mary to rest awhile and then go up to the hedge and pull out a hedge stake. He then beat the poor woman over the head with it. According to Dunkerley's graphic account, the blows sounded like someone hitting a turnip. Then Tom flung down the stake and made off. Dunkerley waited until he was sure the man was not coming back and then went over to examine the woman. He found her dead and he was soon covered in blood as he examined both her and the hedge stake.

He afterwards explained that he didn't come forward immediately because – with blood on his clothes – he was frightened that he might be accused of the murder. He kept quiet even after the trial and the execution because he was ashamed that he might be accused of not going to help the poor woman, when perhaps he might have saved her. Was his account true, or had he made it all up just to court notoriety? Most people seemed to have believed him and indeed my earlier account of the murder is based on his.

The hedge stake was put on display at The Sun Inn in Saxilby, but on the first anniversary of the murder it disappeared from where it hung on the pub wall and was later found in the field where it was first discovered after the murder. This continued to happen in various pubs where it was exhibited along the banks of the Fossdyke, even when it was secured to the wall by metal clasps! It is said that it was finally burnt in Minster Yard on the orders of the Bishop of Lincoln. The gibbet remained there until about 1850, keeping alive the legends that sprang up around the murder of poor Mary by the villain Thomas Otter.

Priscilla Biggadike, 1868

'Do you know the mice have eaten a hole in my flour bag?' said Eliza Fenwick.

'Oh that's awful. Here, let me give you some white mercury. That'll soon see them off.' The speaker was Priscilla Biggadike and she got to her feet from the kitchen table, where they had been sitting, and went to a cupboard. But Mrs Fenwick's husband stopped her.

'I wouldn't have that stuff in my house at any price,' he snapped.

White mercury was the common name at that time for arsenic, often used for killing vermin, impregnating flypapers and even used by some ladies for whitening the skin, which was very fashionable at the time. The exchange took place some time in June 1868 at the home of Priscilla Biggadike in the village of Stickney, six miles from Spilsby and seven from Boston. The house was a very small cottage near the centre of the village and Priscilla, who was twenty-nine, lived there with her thirty-one-year-old husband Richard, two children and a baby, and two lodgers – Thomas Proctor, who was also thirty, and George Ironmonger, aged twenty-one. The house only had two living rooms and sleeping arrangements must have been difficult, with the small bedroom having two beds only 18 inches apart. Richard Biggadike was described as an agricultural labourer and a well-digger, Thomas Proctor was a rat catcher and George Ironmonger, a fisherman.

But what might have been a peaceful family existence was fraught with tension. It could have been the close proximity of the beds, which led to promiscuity, but whatever the reason there is little doubt that at various times Priscilla shared a bed with both Ironmonger and Proctor. It seems though that Proctor was the favourite, which is surprising, since he is described as being of ugly countenance, having a long back and a serious malformation of the legs. Her behaviour caused disruption with Richard, who was suspicious of his wife's activities and firmly believed that the baby was not his. On her part she was antagonistic to him. When she was seen in a new dress, she was at pains to say that it was not bought with her husband's money, and on several occasions neighbours heard her say that she would like to see him brought home dead.

Things reached a crisis point on 30 September 1868. On that day Richard arrived home at about six o'clock. The lodgers had come in an hour earlier and had the same meal as Richard – mutton, oatcakes and tea. Priscilla had made three oatcakes. Two she gave to her lodgers and the third was eaten by Richard. Soon after his meal, he was violently ill, having to rush outside to be sick and to visit the privy, where he was violently purged. This continued throughout the evening and eventually Dr Maxwell was called. He was immediately suspicious, knowing full well the tensions in the house, and he took samples of the food Richard had eaten and of his vomit. He also prescribed a soothing mixture, but he realised that he could not save Richard, who died at about six o'clock the following morning.

Dr Maxwell performed a post-mortem on the body and sent off several samples of the organs to Guy's Hospital in London. He also informed the police in Spilsby of his suspicions. Later at the inquest, which was held in the Rose and Crown, Stickney, Professor Taylor reported that he had examined the samples sent to him and discovered arsenic in every one. He was of the opinion that Richard must have received a large dose on the evening of the 30th. 'I never saw a clearer case of arsenic poisoning,' he said, 'and death took place rather earlier than usual, due to the large dose administered.'

Superintendent Wright of the Spilsby police arrested Priscilla on 3 October and took her to the House of Correction at Spilsby. On the way there she complained that she was taking all the blame for her husband's death. She also said that she had seen a piece of paper in her husband's pocket, which was a confession that he was so heavily in debt that he had committed suicide. The Superintendent pointed out that her husband could not write, so she then said that someone else must have written it for him. When he asked her for the note she said that she had burnt it.

On 15 October, Priscilla made a statement to John Phillips, the governor of the House of Correction at Spilsby:

> On the last day of September on Wednesday I was standing against the tea table and saw Thomas Proctor put a white power of some sort into a teacup and then he poured some milk which stood on the table into it my husband's teacup. At that time he was in the dairy washing himself. My husband came into the room directly after and sat himself down at the table and I then poured his tea and he drank it, and more besides that. And half an hour afterwards he was taken ill . . .

She then went on to describe getting the doctor, who gave her some medicine, two teaspoonfuls to be taken every half an hour. She described going downstairs at some point in the evening and asking Thomas Proctor to sit with her husband:

> When I went upstairs into the bedroom I saw Proctor putting some white powder into the medicine bottle with a spoon and he then left the room and went downstairs. When he had gone I gave some of the medicine to my husband and tasted some myself. An hour afterwards I was sick and so I was for two days afterwards . . .

Priscilla signed the statement with her mark – a cross – as she could not write either.

Both Priscilla and Thomas Proctor went before magistrates at Spilsby and were committed for trial at the Lincolnshire Assizes. The trial began on Friday 11 December. As was usual at the time, a grand jury examined the cases of each of the defendants before passing a true bill against them. It was at this stage that the judge, Mr Justice Byles, advised the grand jury not to find a true bill against Thomas Proctor and he was duly discharged. Priscilla Biggadike, however, went forward to be tried for the murder of Richard Biggadike. She was defended by Mr Lawrence and the prosecution was in the hands of Mr Bristowe and Mr Horace Smith. They were able to bring in many witnesses to testify that Priscilla had wished her husband dead and indeed it was shown that Richard himself, in the throes of his suffering that night due to the poison, had accused his wife of poisoning him and had thrown a cup at her.

But the main plank of the prosecution case was the administration of the poison. Priscilla herself, while accusing Proctor of doctoring the tea and the medicine, had nevertheless helped to administer them to her husband. The judge in his summing up drew attention to Priscilla's different stories and plainly believed she was making them up. The jury drew the same conclusion and, without leaving the courtroom, brought in a verdict of guilty. But they modified this somewhat by accompanying it by a recommendation for mercy. The judge asked on what grounds they made the recommendation and the foreman, after consulting his colleagues, said it was because the evidence was entirely circumstantial. But the judge ignored the recommendation and pronounced the sentence of death.

The sentence was due to be carried out on 28 December. While in prison, the chaplain visited Priscilla many times and enjoined her to confess her sin. But she would not, maintaining right to the end that she was innocent. Even when relatives visited and they too asked her to recant to save her soul, she refused. But she wrote (presumably dictated) a letter to George Ironmonger, asking him to look after her children, as they would soon be orphans. George, much affected by the letter, rushed to the castle prison to see her, but was refused admittance. During the last few days, Priscilla fell into a depression and when she was taken out of the prison to be hanged her final words were: 'All my troubles are over. Shame you're going to hang me. Surely my troubles are over.'

Priscilla Biggadike was the first person to be hanged in Lincoln under the new law which forbade public execution. Instead, she was hanged in front of where the Crown Court building now stands; the hangman was Thomas Askern. He made a botched job of it and Priscilla took several minutes to die. She is buried on the top of the Lucy Tower and her grave can still be seen today.

The final twist in the tale came with the death of Thomas Proctor in 1888. On his deathbed he confessed that he had indeed poisoned both the tea and the medicine which was given to Richard Biggadike.

The Lucy Tower in Lincoln Castle.

Peter Blanchard, 1875

Louth, popularly known as 'the capital of the Wolds', is some 25 miles, as the crows flies, north-east of Lincoln. It lies where an ancient trackway known as Barton Street comes down from the north and crosses the River Lud. Of the buildings in the town the most noteworthy is the parish church of St James, begun in 1441 and completed with its magnificent spire in 1515, which at 295ft (90m) is reputed to be the tallest Anglican parish church in the United Kingdom.

The grammar school in Louth is named after Edward VI, but its origins go back to 1276. Among its famous scholars are Admiral Hobart Pasha (who ran a blockade off North Carolina in the American Civil War), Governor Eyre of Jamaica, Sir John Franklin, who died trying to find the North West Passage, Captain John Smith, first president of Virginia, and the Tennyson brothers. Frederick Tennyson, who was overshadowed by his younger brother Alfred, but still a noted poet, was born in the town in 1807. Other luminaries of the town include Philip Norton, Baron Norton of Louth, and Michael Foale, the first British-born astronaut.

Few people will have heard of the following villain, yet when he took a train journey from Louth to Lincoln, 500 people crowded the small station to watch him depart, and a crowd of sightseers packed every station the train stopped at to catch a glimpse of him. The young man was Peter Blanchard, who was twenty-six in March 1875 and the eldest son of Peter Blanchard, who was a fellmonger – a dealer in skins and hides – and a tanner, and lived in Charles Street, Louth. Peter the younger came from the usual large Victorian family, having four brothers and two sisters, but he did not live in the family home. He had taken lodgings with an elderly and infirm widow, Mrs Elizabeth Baker, who lived in Eastgate.

Peter Blanchard had a chequered career. He had served with the local militia, and he had gone to sea for a period

Louth railway station. (Courtesy Norman Cawkwell)

with the fishing fleet at Grimsby, but for the past few years
he had returned to his hometown and worked for his father
as a tanner. Unfortunately, he was an epileptic. His seizures,
though they were not frequent, were severe and prolonged
and he would sometimes remain unconscious for half an
hour or more. Coupled with this, or maybe because of it,
he had a short and often violent temper. But he had many
friends in Louth and they stood by him and supported
him when necessary. He was also engaged to be married.
His intended was a young woman of twenty-two, Louisa
Armstrong, who lived with her parents in Newmarket. Her
father, John, was an agricultural implement maker and had a
shop in the town.

Although the pair had been 'walking out' for four years,
Louisa's parents were not all that keen on Blanchard as a pro-
spective son-in-law. Possibly it was his propensity to have fits,
or it may have been because of his short temper. Whatever it
was, when a handsome young farmer named John Campion,
who lived on the Brackenborough Road, and was a friend of

one of her brothers, began to take an interest in young Louisa, they welcomed him with open arms. He frequently took tea with the whole family and was looked upon as a far better prospect than the pugnacious Peter.

John Campion took tea with the Armstrongs on Sunday 7 March and then accompanied the family to the Free Methodist Church in Eastgate. He walked behind with Louisa, but when they reached Peter Blanchard's lodgings in Eastgate that gentleman was standing in the doorway. John Armstrong had a word with him in passing but Peter wanted to talk to Louisa. She stopped and so did John Campion, but Blanchard glared at him and he shrugged his shoulders and walked on, but not very far. It was plain that Peter wanted a longer conversation with her, but she did not want to let her family get too far away. Campion, seeing her hesitating, called out, 'Are you coming, Louisa?'

Blanchard immediately shouted back, 'If you tell her to come on while I am talking to her I'll give you a thrashing.'

Free Methodist Church, Louth. (Courtesy Norman Cawkwell)

At this Campion again shrugged his shoulders and went ahead to join the others while Louisa and Blanchard, walking together, brought up the rear. Peter went as far as the church door, but did not go in with the others. Campion and Louisa went in together. Peter Blanchard was waiting for Louisa when the family came out at about 7.30 p.m. John Armstrong had to see some men about church business and he did not arrive at his home until about nine o'clock. He found the family in the kitchen at the back of the house. In the front room Louisa and Peter were talking together. It was dark in the room, but a small window of frosted glass gave a little light from the kitchen behind.

It seems likely at this stage that Louisa was endeavoring to end her association with the young man, but trying to let him down lightly. At all events they were having a long talk, and at times the family in the kitchen could hear Blanchard's raised voice, though they couldn't hear what was being said. Campion decided to leave at about 9.30 p.m., and as he was in the passage leading to the front door he passed the door to the front room. He heard Peter shouting and he thought he heard Louisa crying. However, he did nothing about it and left by the front door. Shortly after ten that night, the family in the kitchen heard more shouting, this time from the passage, and what sounded like scuffling. Then there was a piercing scream from Louisa. John Armstrong rushed out into the passage just in time to see Blanchard leave by the front door, leaving it partly open. Louisa was leaning against the wall holding her hand to her chest and through her fingers blood trickled.

'What is the matter my dear?' John asked.

'Peter,' Louisa gasped for breath. 'He has stabbed me!'

Jane Armstrong, Louisa's mother, pushed forward, wrapped her arms around her daughter and got her into the kitchen. By this time her face was very pale and she was obviously in a fainting condition. She collapsed onto the lap of one of her brothers.

Newmarket, Louth. (Courtesy Norman Cawkwell)

'Where has he stabbed you?' asked Mrs Armstrong.

'In the heart,' mumbled Louisa. She was losing consciousness fast.

John Armstrong raced out of his house. Blanchard had disappeared by this time and the distraught father first went for medical assistance and then for the police. Dr Thomas Higgins arrived at the Armstrong house in Newmarket at a little after ten o'clock. He found that poor Louisa was already dead. At the subsequent post-mortem, which he conducted the next day, he found that Louisa had suffered just one stab wound. Unfortunately, the weapon had penetrated the chest wall, gone between the fourth and fifth ribs, sliced through the left lung and entered the left side of the heart. There was very little external bleeding, since most of it was internal, and she would have died within minutes.

Sometime after ten that Sunday night, William Turner, a poulterer, was sitting by the fire in his house in Vickers Lane. He was dozing, but woke up when he heard someone trying the front door, which was locked. 'Who is it?' he called.

A hoarse voice answered, 'It's me, Peter.'

Turner got up, went to the front door and unlocked it. Outside stood Peter Blanchard, looking haggard and panting hard. 'Let me in,' he gasped, 'and give me some whisky.'

The poulterer stood aside and let the shaking young man come in. He was himself middle-aged, but had known Peter Blanchard since the young man was a boy. Indeed, Peter was now lodging with Turner's mother, Mrs Elizabeth Baker.

'Can you let me have a little whiskey, William?' asked Peter again.

'I don't know if we've got any,' answered the poulterer. 'I'd ask the wife, but she's gone to bed.'

'Please William. I really need some.'

Turner saw that the young man was extremely agitated and he went to the bottom of the stairs and called to his wife. Harriet Turner came downstairs, bleary eyed and in her dressing gown. 'Whatever's the matter, William?'

Her husband explained the situation to her. 'Well,' she said doubtfully, 'we haven't any whisky, but I think we've got some brandy, if that will do?' She looked across at Blanchard. 'You do look awful Peter. What is the matter?'

The young man hung his head, but answered Turner. 'I've done it William!'

'Good Heavens. Done what?'

'I've stabbed the missus.'

'Stabbed the missus? Who do you mean?'

'Louisa Armstrong.'

'Oh my God! What did you do it with?'

'With a butcher's knife. But I've thrown it away. And if I hadn't that I would have used this.' He fumbled in his pocket and produced a cut-throat razor of the type which folds into the handle. Opening it up he began waving it about.

'Peter,' said Harriet, 'be careful, you might cut yourself. Why don't you give the razor to William?'

The young man nodded and folded the razor up and handed it over. William could see that Blanchard was in a very excitable condition, but he couldn't quite accept what the young man was telling him. Such a thing was unthinkable in a small community like this. And in any case he didn't want to shoulder the responsibility of handling the situation himself. He therefore roused his eldest son and told him to go to Blanchard's parent's house in Charles Street and bring them back with him. Then he gave Peter some brandy, sat him at the table and tried to pacify him.

When Peter's parents arrived, Turner explained the situation to them and then sent his eldest son on another errand. He was to go to the Armstrong house in Newmarket and see if what Peter was saying was true. He took the boy to one side and told him privately that if it was true he was to go and report the matter to Sergeant John Wilkinson.

The result was that subsequently Sergeant Wilkinson arrived at the Turner house in Vickers Lane, accompanied by his superior, Superintendent Roberts. The Sergeant went in ahead of the Superintendent into the crowded room. He estimated later that there were a dozen or fourteen people crowded into the small space. Immediately Peter Blanchard, who had been sitting at a table, saw him he jumped up. 'Is she dead, John?'

'I'm afraid she is. You'll have to come with us Peter.' He produced a pair of handcuffs from his pocket. Blanchard's mother screamed and burst into tears and the young man moaned, 'Oh no, not the handcuffs.'

'I'm afraid we shall have to do this,' said the Superintendent, 'because you will be charged with killing Louisa Armstrong.' The two officers manacled the young man and took him outside into the street. A crowd had already collected, but that didn't prevent Blanchard shouting, 'It's a good job! I'm dammed glad I did it!' The Superintendent cautioned him not to say anything further and they took him to the police station. But even there he couldn't keep quiet and after he had been cautioned and placed in a cell, he asked to see Sergeant Wilkinson, whom he knew, and said to him, 'This is real love you know. When a fellow will die for a girl.'

Blanchard had thrown away the knife on his way to Vickers Lane and Sergeant Wilkinson found it at the top of Aswell Street, opposite the Boar's Head public house. The inquest opened the following day, at the Boar's Head, but the pub turned out to be too small to accommodate the large number of people wanting to attend and the inquest was moved to the Town Hall. There, after evidence had been taken and witnesses had been examined, the jury brought in a verdict of willful murder against Peter Blanchard. The next day, before the magistrates he was committed for trial at the Lincoln Assizes. He left by the 6.34 a.m. train for Lincoln and his departure was witnessed by some 500 people, for this was a local sensation – the local paper estimated that there had not been a murder in the town for a hundred years.

Peter Blanchard's trial took place on Friday, 23 July 1875 at Lincoln, before Mr Justice Lindley. Mr H. Smith and Mr Holloway appeared for the prosecution and Mr Waddy defended. The prosecution case was straightforward; there was the evidence of witnesses that he had admitted to the crime, and the evidence of the now deceased Louisa that he

Louth Town Hall. (Courtesy Norman Cawkwell)

had stabbed her. Insanity was the only defence offered by Mr
Waddy. Dr Higgins, the local Louth doctor, said that epilepsy
was a frequent cause of insanity, but he hesitated to say that
a person committing a crime of this sort was insane because
he was suffering from the disease. The defence also called no
evidence to show insanity in the accused family. The judge
summed up and the jury did not leave the box, bringing in a
verdict of guilty of murder in less than fifteen minutes.

It is interesting to consider that only a year later, William
Drant of Hemingby was also convicted of murder after clubbing
a man to death, but he was reprieved after a petition was raised
in the village and it was reported that he was suffering from
epilepsy. Peter Blanchard was not so lucky. He was condemned
to death and was hanged in private in the castle yard by executioner Marwood on Monday 9 August. A large crowd gathered
outside the castle in the pouring rain to wait for the black flag
to be raised, indicating that the execution had been carried out.

Executioner Marwood.
(Courtesy Richard D'Arcy)

David Dennis, 1958

Scredington is a village just off the A15 Sleaford to Bourne road, some three and a half miles from Sleaford itself. It's a small place and looks the typical sleepy village that one finds so often in rural parts of Lincolnshire. It has a pretty collection of bungalows and cottages lining the main street and has a two-arched packhorse bridge, while the church of St Andrew's, with its slender spire and narrow thirteenth-century doorway, pokes its head above the trees. You would never believe that such a calm and peaceful place hides a secret so terrible that few people today will talk about it.

In February 1958, there lived in the village a retired blacksmith whose name was John Spriggs. He was seventy years old and he lived with his sixty-nine-year-old wife, Florence, in a house called Stone Croft Cottage, which stood on the main road into the village. John Spriggs kept himself busy by having a petrol pump at the side of the house and also selling cigarettes from his back door. Round about the 16th of that month, he and his wife disappeared. A sixteen-year-old boy called at the cottage on that day and knocked on the back door. It was opened by a youth not much older than the lad himself, whom he recognised as the couple's grandson, who lived away, but often visited them.

'Sorry,' said the grandson, whose name was David Dennis, 'grandpa and grandma have gone away on holiday.'

The youth asked if David could sell him some cigarettes and the grandson agreed, and the transaction was completed without further ado. In fact, David sold cigarettes and petrol to several people during the following days and told all of them that his grandparents had gone on holiday. He even put a notice on the front door of the cottage saying that his grandparents would be back on 1 March. But the villagers noticed that David seemed to be living at Stone Croft Cottage and not only that but he had his girlfriend living with him. Joan

Robinson was the same age as David, who was only eighteen, and the villagers began to talk amongst themselves. Did the Spriggs know that their grandson was living with a woman in their house? This was a small village and most of the villagers knew each other. Most of them, including the Spriggs, were regular churchgoers and would not have approved of such goings-on.

David Dennis's mother, who lived in Nottingham, was also concerned about her mother and father's disappearance. She used to receive a weekly letter from her mother, but recently she hadn't received any. She wrote to her son David, who told her that John and Florence had gone to Brighton for a holiday, but he would contact them and get his grandmother to write to her. But no letter arrived from Mrs Spriggs.

On 24 February, Dennis went to the Midland Bank in Sleaford and produced a cheque signed J.T. Spriggs for £100 and made out to bearer. The bank duly paid up. A few days later he returned with another cheque for £100, again made out to bearer. Again the bank paid up. But the villagers were becoming concerned about the continued occupation of Stone Croft Cottage by the couple and they contacted the police. But the police merely put them down on the missing persons list and suggested that they would soon turn up. But early on 7 March, villagers saw David and his girlfriend loading up Mr and Mrs Spriggs' Austen A30 car with suitcases and household items and then driving off. Someone rapidly got in touch with the police. The police had now heard about the bank withdrawals and they were suspicious too. So, later that day, a Superintendent and several police officers broke into the cottage.

The sight that met their eyes was appalling. In the dining room, which had the curtains drawn since it looked out on to the street, lay the body of John Spriggs. He had been battered to death with a poker. Upstairs in the bathroom they found Florence. She had been similarly attacked and lay dead upon the floor. A general alert was put out for the couple and for the car. It was soon spotted in Hampstead and the couple were arrested in a flat nearby. They were taken to the local police station, where David immediately confessed to murdering his grandparents and forging their signatures. He was brought to trial on 2 June at Lincoln Assizes.

Young Joan claimed that she knew nothing about the murders, having arrived at the cottage after they were committed, and David kept her out of the rooms where the bodies lay. She also said that she did not realise that the property they had removed from the house had been stolen. This was accepted by the courts and the charges against her were dropped. But David Dennis, on the other hand, faced execution. In 1957, a new Homicide Act came into force. There had been considerable moves previous to this to get rid of the death penalty for murder and the new Act was a compromise. If it could be shown that murder had been committed during the furtherance of a felony, or if a policeman had been killed, then that was capital murder and the sentence was death. If the murder was committed without a felony being perpetrated, then it was non-capital murder and the sentence was life imprisonment. So, if it could be shown that David murdered his grandparents in order to steal their car, it would be capital murder.

On the second day of the trial David dismissed his counsel (although he retained the services of his solicitor), and conducted the defence himself. He claimed that the murders had arisen through a quarrel and he had no intention at the time of stealing the car. He had been in trouble with the police and was accused of burgling a shop in Brighton. His grandparents, who had doted on him before, now said they wanted nothing further to do with him and he had lost his temper and attacked them. Although the judge had earlier cautioned him against conducting his defence himself, he was obviously impressed with the young man's performance in court and summed up in his favour. The jury took the hint and convicted him only of non-capital murder. David Dennis was sentenced to life imprisonment. He served fourteen years.

Bibliography

Books

Abbott, Geoffrey, *Lords of the Scaffold*, Headline Book Publishing, 1992

Bernard Wood, G., *Smugglers' Britain*, Cassell, 1966

Conway-Walter, James, *Mablethorpe: Its History and Associations*, Wiggen Brothers

Davey, B.J., *Rural Crime in the Eighteenth Century*, The University of Hull Press, 1994

Evans, Hilary and Mary, *Hero on a Stolen Horse*, Frederick Muller Ltd, 1997

Finger, Charles J., *Highwaymen*, Books for the Libraries Press, 1970

Gagen, N.V., *Hanged at Lincoln (1716-1961)*, Private Publication

Gillett, Edward, *A History of Grimsby*, Oxford University Press, 1970

Gillett, Edward and MacMahon, Kenneth A., *A History of Hull*, The University of Hull Press, 1989

Gray, Adrian, *Crime and Criminals in Victorian Lincolnshire*, Paul Watkins, 1993

Gray, Adrian, *Lincolnshire Tales of Mystery and Murder*, Countryside Books, 2004

Gurnham, Richard, *A History of Lincoln*, Phillimore & Co. Ltd, 2009

Haining, Peter, *The English Highwayman*, Robert Hale, 1991

Hill, Sir Francis, *A Short History of Lincoln*, Lincoln Civic Trust, 1979

Hodgett, Gerald A.J., *Tudor Lincolnshire*, History of Lincolnshire Committee, 1975

Holmes, Clive, *Seventeenth-Century Lincolnshire*, History of Lincolnshire Committee, 1980

Holmes, Neil, *The Lawless Coast*, Larks Press, 2009

Jackson, Peter Norman and Jackson, Elaine, *The Life of Dick Turpin*, Arthur H. Stockwell Ltd, 1988

La Bern, Arthur, *Haigh*, W.H. Allen, 1973

Mathews, Derek, *William Marwood*, Fastprint Publishing, 2010

Morland, Nigel, *Hangman's Clutch*, Werner Laurie, 1954

Murray, Jim, *Tealby Gleanings*, Bayons Books, 1995

Painter, Bill, *The Story of Louth House of Correction*, Louth Naturalists', Antiquarian and Literary Society, 2004

Pierrepoint, Albert, *Executioner: Pierrepoint*, George G. Harrap and Co. Ltd, 1974

Platt, Richard, *Smuggling in the British Isles*, Tempus, 2007

Robertson, Stuart (ed.), *The Pirates Pocket-Book*, Conway, 2008

Robinson, David N., *The Book of the Lincolnshire Seaside*, Baron Books, 1989

Robinson, David N., *Adam Eve and Louth Carpets*, Louth Naturalists, Antiquarian and Literary Society, 2010

Robinson B.A. and Robinson F.W., *History of Long Sutton and District*, Long Sutton and District Society, 1986

Rogers, Alan, *A History of Lincolnshire*, Phillimore & Co. Ltd, 1985

Southworth, Pamela, *Delaney The Cat Burglar*, Richard Kay, 2005

Wade, Stephen, *Lincolnshire Murders*, Sutton Publishing, 2006

Wade, Stephen, *Foul Deeds & Suspicious Deaths in Grimsby and Cleethorpes*, Wharncliffe Books, 2007

Webb, Duncan, *Crime is my Business*, Frederick Muller, 1953

Wilson, Colin, Wilson Damon & Wilson Rowan, *World Famous Robberies*, Magpie, 1994

Wynn, Douglas, *Murder & Crime: Lincolnshire*, The History Press, 2009

Wynn, Douglas, *Murder & Crime: Boston*, The History Press, 2010

Newspapers

Boston Gazette

Lincolnshire Chronicle

Lincoln Rutland and Stamford Mercury

Louth and North Lincolnshire Advertiser

Scunthorpe Evening Telegraph

The Epworth Bells

If you enjoyed this book, you may also be interested in …

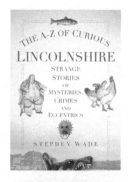

The A-Z of Curious Lincolnshire

STEPHEN WADE

This book is filled with hilarious and surprising examples of folklore, historical and literary events, and popular culture from days gone by. Meet poets, aristocrats, politicians and some less likely residents of the county, including Spring-Heeled Jack. This is the county that brought us Lord Tennyson (whose brother was treated at an experimental asylum in the area), and, in contrast, William Marwood, the notorious hangman.

978 0 7524 6027 7

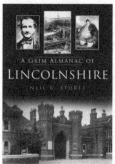

A Grim Almanac of Licolnshire

NEIL R. STOREY

A day-by-day catalogue of 365 ghastly tales from around the county dating from the twelfth to the twentieth centuries. Full of dreadful deeds, macabre deaths, strange occurrences and heinous homicides, this compilation contains such diverse tales of highwaymen, smugglers, bodysnatchers, poachers, witches, rioters and rebels, as well as accounts of old lock-ups, prisons, and punish-ments as well as tales of murder, suicide, and much more.

978 0 7524 5768 0

Folklore of Lincolnshire

SUSANNA O'NEILL

Home to a wealth of folklore, legend and intrigue, this vast region is also rich in superstitions, songs and traditional games. A study of the daily life, lore and customs of Lincolnshire are here interspersed with stories of monstrous black hounds, dragon lairs, witches, Tiddy Mun, mischievous imps and tales of the people known as the Yellowbellies.

978 0 7524 5964 6

Visit our website and discover thousands of other History Press books.

www.thehistorypress.co.uk